Two Yachts, Two Voyages

By the same author:

Wandering Under Sail
Cruising Under Sail
Around the World in *Wanderer III*
Beyond the West Horizon
Atlantic Cruise in *Wanderer III*
Sou'west in *Wanderer IV*
Come Aboard

Two Yachts, Two Voyages

ERIC C. HISCOCK

W · W · NORTON & COMPANY
New York   London

First American Edition, 1985

ISBN 0-393-03307-4

W. W. Norton & Company, Inc., 500 Fifth Avenue, New York, N.Y. 10110
W. W. Norton & Company Ltd., 37 Great Russell Street, London WC1B 3NU

Book-of-the-Month Records® offers a wide range of
opera, classical and jazz recordings. For information and
catalog write to BOMR, Camp Hill, PA 17012.

For
Frank Eyre

Contents

Acknowledgements

The acknowledgements of the author are due to the Editors of *Cruising World*, *Yachting Monthly* and *Yachting World*, in which magazines some parts of this story were first published.

Two Yachts, Two Voyages

PART I
Voyage to British Columbia

It was early April, beginning of the southern winter, yet for the past three months the wind had blown from the easterly quarter with a constancy suggesting that New Zealand lay not in the variables but in the trade wind belt, and it was still in the east, a headwind for us. However, Susan (my wife) and I wanted to get away before the winter gales arrived and to reach our final destination before the heavy fogs of the late northern summer set in. So, having obtained our outward clearance, we spent one final peaceful night at anchor and put to sea next day.

The idea of sailing our 49-foot steel ketch *Wanderer IV* from New Zealand, which had been her base for the past 18 months, to the west coast of Canada had been in our minds for some time, indeed ever since we were last in England, for while in the Falmouth area we had met two Canadian couples, Tom and Margaret Denny, and Steve and Esther Dickinson. The Dennys had recently bought a Moody-built Carbineer, *Daphne Isle*, and were about to sail her out to their home waters. They gave us *Victoria Calling*, a book of colour photographs showing the charms of that city, and on the end paper Tom drew a little map showing the position of a small island he and Margaret owned. He told us it had a house, a workshop and a well-sheltered float where *Wanderer* could lie safely, and if we ever went to British Columbia we were to use the island as though it were our own. The Dickinsons were in *Kapduva*, a big Garden-designed ketch which they had sailed from Hong Kong. They, too, had property near Victoria, notably a large marina at Sydney. 'If you ever sail out there we will always find you a berth.'

Such invitations are not easily dismissed, but Susan and I did not make our final decision to go until, after returning to New Zealand, we were invited to dine aboard the Canadian trimaran *Tryste II* by our world-girdling friends Ernest and Val Haigh. As we sat round their cabin table bathed in the low, evening sunlight, they showed us charts and told us a little about their home waters, which in the shelter of big Vancouver Island thread their way among countless tree-clad islands, and of the great, crooked, fiord-like fingers which thrust in among snow-topped mountains. They told us, too, of salmon and eagles and great rafts of logs, but they made light of the approach through the notoriously foggy Strait of Juan de Fuca.

As we made our preparations the old familiar, exciting sense of keen anticipation made itself felt, for once again we were to experience the exquisite satisfaction of sailing our own ship across great expanses of ocean, the success of the venture depending on her integrity and that of her gear, and on our own resources, knowing that anything we might have neglected or forgotten would have to be improvised or done without, and at the end to reach a land entirely new to us.

When we wrote to our Canadian friends to say we were coming their response was immediate and touching. Tom sent us some essential charts and tide tables and outlined a plan for *Daphne Isle* and *Wanderer IV* to cruise in company. Steve sent some local knowledge about the approaches, and thoughtfully enclosed several dimes so that we could telephone on arrival, and the Greys, retired farmers, sent a cable which read: 'Have good hitching-post and water-trough.'

The voyage of about 7,000 miles would take us across the Pacific from south to north, something we had not attempted before though we had crossed that great ocean in other directions on several occasions with the wind abaft the beam. This time the wind would probably be forward of the beam most of the way, and we could expect to be hard on the wind for a considerable part of the distance, so although we might be wet and uncomfortable, at least we would sail a little faster than when running. We planned to make only two stops: at Tahiti in the Society Islands and at Hilo in Hawaii. This would split the voyage into three passages of almost equal length, each one

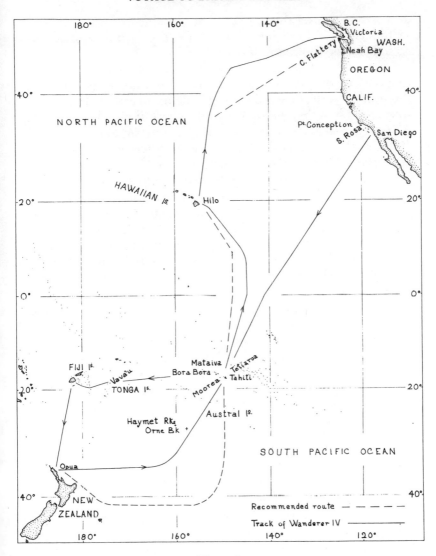

Chart A

only a trifle shorter than an Atlantic crossing from the Canaries to the West Indies. See Chart A for the recommended and actual routes of *Wanderer IV*.

Of course one can sail direct from New Zealand to Tahiti, that is along the great circle track, but this is taking a gamble on the south-east trade wind having little or no east in it, or on its southern boundary being north of where it should be. *Ocean Passages for the World* recommends that one should go south of 40°S to take advantage of the prevailing westerlies there and not edge away to the northward until in 155°W. However we thought so high a latitude might be too cold and windy for us, and decided instead to steer a middle course in 30°S to 35°S where, in the variables between the trade wind and the westerlies, we could expect winds from any direction so at least some of them should be favourable, and not to head for Tahiti until we were confident of being able to fetch that island on the starboard tack. This would mean sailing a greater distance than if we kept to the great circle track, though not so great as if we followed the recommended route. But in the event it would have made little difference (apart from distance) which route we took, for at the time easterly winds prevailed over much of the South Pacific, even extending high into the forties; as a result we were closehauled nearly all the way, and at times had to beat to windward. Often the weather was cold and damp, and the cabin sole remained dark with wet for the first two weeks. We had only one strong gale, which was from ahead, and caused some havoc among the yachts in the place we had recently left. It was ushered in by a splendid dawn rainbow, and later so heavily overcast was the sky and so solid the driving rain that I needed a light at the chart table when writing up the log at noon.

On our fourteenth day at sea we started to edge nor'east towards Tahiti, and a little later passed south of two vigias: Orne Bank and Haymet Rocks. The former was reported in 1874 by the French transport *Orne* when she passed over and apparently touched a bank on which a depth of 16 fathoms with rocky bottom was obtained almost immediately afterwards. Thirteen years later a search was made for this bank over a considerable area by the French warship *Fahert*, but she only succeeded in obtaining soundings of 34 fathoms about eight miles eastward of the reported position; then in 1938 the SS *City of Canberra* sounded across the charted position of the bank but obtained no indication of it. Haymet Rocks were reported in 1863 by the master of the cutter *Will Watch*. He stated that his vessel passed between two rocks and struck on the northern one damaging her false keel; the rocks were distinctly seen and extended over a space of about a quarter of a mile with depths estimated at from seven to eight feet over them. Unsuccessful searches were made for these rocks by HMS *Satellite* in 1886 and by *Fahert* a year later, the latter searching for three days within a radius of 25 miles of the position originally reported. Clearly these vigias, if in fact they exist, do not lie in their charted positions, so we gave the latter a very wide berth.

After that the weather improved, growing warmer and drier and the sea ran more easily. I thought one evening as I lay on my back on the foredeck watching the stars wheel overhead and listening to the steady rush of the bow wave, how fortunate I was to be there to enjoy it, and Susan had a similar feeling the next morning when she saw a brilliant green flash as the sun rose. To see an evening green flash is commonplace, but in the morning it is difficult because one cannot tell on exactly which part of the horizon to fix one's unwinking eye. We saw only one ship, but with the vane gear doing all the steering we did not keep much of a look-out in those lonely waters.

We slanted up through the Austral group without sighting any of them, and dawn on our twenty-seventh day at sea showed the misty peaks of Tahiti ahead. We knew all about the calms which plague the channel between Tahiti and neighbouring Moorea, so to hold our wind we should have passed to windward of Tahiti to reach Papeete, which port lies on that island's northern shore; but that would have added extra miles to our already over-long passage, and we reckoned we could easily motor through the channel, which we proceeded to do immediately we lost the wind. With no wind to steady her, *Wanderer* rolled abominably in the beam swell, and later she started to plunge into a steep headsea; that should have warned us of what was to come. Hour after hour we plugged slowly on and had reached a position only five miles short of Papeete Pass when a wind of gale force sprang at us from dead ahead. It soon became clear that under power or sail or both we were not going to make port before nightfall, and not wishing to enter in the dark because of the likely difficulty of finding a berth in that usually crowded place, we bore away and had a wild, wet, high-speed reach across to Moorea, where we found absolute peace in glorious Cook Bay near a party of small German yachts. A friendly dinghy-load at once rowed over from them with presents of bread, fruit, *corones* of fresh flowers including *tiare Tahiti* (the South Sea gardenia with the heady, never-to-be-forgotten perfume) and a bottle of cool wine, 'Because,' they said, 'you have been here so often.' Such kindness!

Moorea is not a port of entry, but the *gendarme* allowed us to remain over the weekend, after which we went to Papeete to enter. As we approached the pass which was flanked on its eastern side by a massive new breakwater standing on the reef, another German yacht which we had met on an earlier occasion was coming in too. Her owners, Horst and Tilly, who had been at Tahiti for a year and knew it well, indicated a suitable berth for us in front of the conspicuous red and white Protestant church, and by the time we had let go and veered cable they had launched their dinghy to take our stern lines to rocks on the shore. They were helpful to us in other ways, collecting a roll of charts from the parcel office, which was not where one might have expected to find it in the town but across at the far side of the harbour, and Horst took our 20-lb gas bottle on his back and cycled with it through the snarling traffic to get it filled.

For yachts Papeete is the crossroads of the South Pacific, and it is the voyaging people one meets there that makes it so fascinating, not the town which on this visit had even less charm than it had the last time we were there, as much of it has been rebuilt in modern style and it was overburdened with fast motor traffic.

After two days at Papeete we returned to the peace and beauty of Moorea for a short time, and chose an anchorage where the shadow cast by a nearby mountain provided a long, cool evening twilight, and at the ferry wharf we filled our tanks with pure, soft water. A Tahitian woman in the *buvette* close by lent us a long hose, for the tap was at the root of the wharf, and when Susan returned it she offered a small present—this was declined, and a freshly-caught fish was pressed smilingly into Susan's hands.

The success under sail of a passage between the Society Islands and Hawaii largely depends on crossing the equator far enough up-wind, i.e. to the east, so that later, when the north-east trade wind is met with, the destination can be fetched with sheets eased a little. *Ocean Passages* recommends 148°W as a suitable longitude, but we felt that might be cutting it fine and decided to cross in 145°W. Possibly Peter and Anne Pye in *Moonraker*, when they made this passage in 1953, had the same feeling, for although they left from Bora Bora, which is 130 miles to leeward of Moorea, they crossed the equator in 145°W.

We had expected this trade wind passage to be enjoyable, but the first part of it was not. The day before we were due to leave Moorea an American friend took us for a drive round that attractive island (partly so that we might lay in a supply of *pamplemousse*, a citrus bigger and better than a grapefruit), and we saw that a heavy sea was breaking on the barrier reef all along the island's north and east sides, and everybody reckoned it was *mauvais temps*.

Next morning was calm and we motored away into a vile headsea, finding the wind an hour later. Unfortunately this had no south but a lot of north in it, so again we were closehauled just as we had been most of the way from New Zealand. It was mid-May when we set out, and the pilot chart for that month showed the wind averaging only Force 3, but with us it was between Force 5 and 7, and life on board was wet and uncomfortable, and much too hot and stuffy down below. Normally *Wanderer*'s aft to forward natural ventilation was good, but now we needed the hood up over the fore part of the cockpit, and this competed with the partly open forehatch in trying to suck air from below, with the result that there was a pocket of dead air in the saloon where we lived and slept. The temptation to bear away a little and ease sheets was great, but we were set on crossing the line in 145°W, even though we did have to beat to windward for two miserable days to do so. That was a point of sailing *Wanderer* hated almost as much as we did, and we found it was best to regard her as a square-rigger rather than a fore-and-after, and attempt to sail no closer than six points to the wind except in smooth water, so naturally a beat to windward was a slow and unrewarding business. Meanwhile there was no opportunity to dry the laundry which Susan had done at Moorea, and the wet towels, which perhaps had not been properly rinsed, smelt like over-ripe cheese.

It was something of a relief to come at last to the doldrum belt, which turned out to be about 100 miles wide, and without hesitation we started up the Ford diesel and motored clean through it. No doubt this was cheating, but having crossed the equator and the doldrums seven times before and mostly under sail alone, we felt entitled to make the affair as easy and painless as possible on this occasion. The sea was astonishingly steep and confused, the sort of thing that may be found in the Race of Alderney, and we supposed this might be due to the currents, notably the east-running Counter Current, although we were unable to detect more than half a knot of it. Incidentally, *Pacific Islands Pilot*, Volume III, which covers these waters, states that there are no doldrums and that the one trade wind changes to the other almost imperceptibly. Thereafter we had more comfortable sailing, and headed at first for a point well to windward of Hawaii to allow for the west-setting North Equatorial Current, but bore away a bit when we found that the current did no more than about five miles a day. Under a clear sky with gentler motion and less spray flying, we were able to open the galley skylight for better ventilation, and through it watch from below the silent, power-filled curves of the sails, their tan colour contrasting pleasantly with the blue overhead.

Navigation in such conditions was easy and I could choose my own time for taking sights, checking our track in the morning by observing the sun when on the beam, and our progress with a noon latitude sight, and at dusk Susan confirmed my position with a round of star observations. When one evening, shortly after crossing the equator, we checked the compass by taking an amplitude we had a pleasant surprise. In the southern hemisphere the compass had seven degrees of westerly deviation on a north-west heading, but now that we were back once more in the northern hemisphere the compass had no deviation on that heading nor, as we subsequently discovered when we swung using a pair of leading beacons at Hilo, any noticeable deviation on any other heading; so it had resumed the stable condition originally imparted to it by Mr Robinson, the Hamble compass-adjuster. This was extraordinary, for so far as I am aware a crossing of the equator, or the magnetic equator, which in the central Pacific almost coincide, should have no effect on a compass except perhaps for heeling error, but steel vessels do present magnetic problems unknown to those built of wood or grp.

Twenty days out of Moorea (2,525 miles) we sighted Hawaii. This is the largest of the Hawaiian Islands, being twice the area of all the others combined, but it is disappointing when viewed from the sea, for although it rises to a height of nearly 14,000 feet the land slopes so gently from the sea to the volcanic peaks that the impact is lost. At Hilo, on the island's eastern side, we passed in behind the mile-long rubble breakwater and came to the pleasant little harbour at its inner end where we anchored, among other ocean voyaging yachts, took a sternline to the shore, and were quickly entered by one of the most courteous and friendly customs officers we had ever had the pleasure of meeting. We remained for five days, doing the washing in a convenient laundromat, watering, provisioning and attending to our ship's requirements, then departed on the final and the most interesting leg of the voyage, heading towards Victoria, British Columbia.

On this passage there are two major considerations: the northern extent of the north-east trade wind and the position of the North Pacific high pressure area. The trade will probably compel one to steer more or less north until it expires, and the 'high', if one is able to alter course towards the land and does so too soon, may keep one becalmed for many days. In June, when we were making the trip, the recommended procedure was to head north until, in about 36°N, the westerlies would be met with, then to turn and steer for the destination. And there were some other things over which one had no control—the likelihood of encountering fog and large fleets of fishing vessels as the land is approached, as well as floating or water-logged timber which could be a serious danger for a small vessel.

We had a powerful east-nor'east trade wind when we left Hilo, and sailing as usual a little free made good 966 miles in the first week. But at 36°N there was no sign of the westerlies, the east-nor'easter continuing unabated, and even at 40°N the conditions were just the same. By then it was growing cold and we were glad of the diesel cabin-heater, and we did not take our socks off day or night; the sky had become overcast and remained so for the rest of the passage; the sea had a grey-brown sullen look, and often there was a chill, penetrating drizzle. Not until we had reached 44°N did the wind die, and then the Leach's and fork-tailed storm-petrels and the black-footed albatrosses, which had been with us ever since the weather became cooler, were able to come right alongside without fear to accept, with apparent pleasure, the lumps of cooking fat and scraps of scrambled egg we offered them. They were all remarkably well-mannered; nobody snatched or squabbled, and the big, benign albatrosses sat and watched but did not interfere with their tiny, fluttering companions. On two successive mornings, while becalmed at breakfast time, Susan was able to feed the chicks. Meanwhile the barograph had risen to a phenomenal height, and for a time stood at 1050 mb (30.75 in), the highest it had ever been in its 20 years of seafaring. So instead of circumnavigating the 'high' as we had hoped, we must have passed through it, yet in all we had no more than about 24 hours of calm.

Naturally we expected the wind to come from a westerly quarter after the calm, but it did not; although it no longer blew from east-nor'east it was still a little east of north, so again we were closehauled, but now on the port tack, and at last were able to head for Cape Flattery, the southern entrance point of Juan de Fuca Strait, about 1,000 miles distant.

Navigation became something of a problem, for in the final two weeks of this passage we saw stars only on one occasion when it was too rough to make use of them, and we never got so much as a glimpse of the waxing and waning moon. So we had only the sun to serve us and, because of the continuous overcast sky, that body was visible only faintly and momentarily on rare occasions; no longer was I able to choose my own time for taking sights but often had to wait a long while on deck in oilskins, sextant in hand, so as to miss no chance of a quick snapshot if the opportunity should offer. So faint was the sun that no index shade was needed on the sextant, and sometimes when the sun could just be seen there was no horizon because of mist. The yacht with radio aids is at an advantage here, for the area is well covered by Loran, and as the coast is approached there are many radio beacons, some with a range of 100 miles, from which to obtain a fix. Apart from a receiving set and echo sounder we had no electronic equipment, but we reasoned that as earlier navigators such as Cook, Vancouver, Pye and Smeeton had managed with Nature's gifts alone so perhaps might we.

Two nights before we were expecting to make a landfall we were reaching at seven knots under very reduced sail with a Force 9 gale blowing from the north. As we had shipped no heavy water I suggested that we remove the washboard from the companionway and leave the door open so as to make it easier and quieter for the watchkeeper to get in and out every ten minutes. I did this, but Susan thought it a poor idea and she was soon proved right, for at about midnight we did ship a heavy crest in the cockpit and this rushed in a torrent down into the saloon with considerable force, swamping the whole of the lee side where it filled the chart stowage and bookshelves, poured into the chest-of-drawers in which we kept the ship's papers, passports, first-aid gear and unanswered letters, all of which were afloat, and it buried under a foot or so of water the lee settee on which I was asleep. We spent the rest of the night pumping out and mopping up and trying to salvage the more important things such as the nautical almanac and books of tables. Needless to say we kept the washboard in and the door tight shut thereafter, but we shipped no more heavy water.

The contrasts of cruising are indeed remarkable. The following evening the sea was smooth and we lay becalmed on La Perouse Bank in company with a fleet of salmon trollers. At nightfall they all stopped fishing, switched on masthead strobe lights, and presumably went to bed, a sensible example that we quickly followed; we felt we were part of a rather exclusive floating village, and it was good to have human neighbours after being so long on our own. We were so impressed by the

eye-catching high intensity of the fishermen's lights that we
determined to fit one one day, and did so when our next boat
was being built; but at about that time such lights were frowned
upon by the international regulations on the grounds that they
might be mistaken for some aid to navigation such, for example, as a north cardinal mark. This, however, will not deter
us from using ours in circumstances where there is no other
means of attracting attention and thus perhaps avoiding being
run down.

We were fortunate to have no thick fog in this particularly
foggy area, and about noon next day made a landfall on Cape
Flattery, which was so named by Cook when he came this way
in March, 1778. But instead of continuing to Victoria, then
only 60 miles farther on, we put in at Neah Bay close to Flattery
on the U.S. side of the strait, and spent the following sunny day
there drying some of our belongings, notably a hundred books
and twice that number of charts that were soaked with
seawater.

Although it was hazy as we made our way up the strait we
could see snow patches on the Olympic mountains, but there
was little wind, and as we could not have reached Victoria in
time to go through customs that day, we put in 10 miles short of
that port at Pedder Bay, passing inside Race Rocks to reach it,
and were swept quickly by on the six knot flood.

Race Rocks, the southernmost portion of Canada west of
Ontario, has been the scene of at least 35 shipwrecks. The
graceful black and white striped lighthouse which surmounts
them is of granite blocks, each one cut, fitted and numbered
before being brought out from England in 1858, and it was one
of the first to be erected in British Columbia. Soon after we had
brought up we were visited by Trev Anderson, the lighthouse
keeper, and his wife Flo in their Boston whaler, for they had
seen *Wanderer* sail past that afternoon and recognized her from a
photograph. They had been on the rock for 12 years, and had
come to invite us to go out there for a visit, which we could not
then do because we had not yet been entered by customs. The
major undertaking they were then engaged on was the building
of a 42-foot wood ketch, not on some sheltered plot of land
ashore, but out there on top of the rock close to the keeper's

house all among the seals, sealions and birds, in the open and fully exposed to the violent winds which so often blow there. Three years later we were to hear from them that the yacht was complete and launched; they had retired from lighthouse keeping and were living aboard.

Arrival at a strange port is always exciting, particularly so when the harbour is as small and busy as that of Victoria. As we came in round the first blind corner with wharves on either side we were overtaken by a large and impatient ferry. We waited for her to berth and then crept on under engine (fortunately there was no wind to complicate matters) until we saw the customs float. But this became obscured by a barge with grabs on it moving out from some hidden recess; meanwhile a float plane had landed astern and was noisily breathing down our necks. Presently the barge moved clear, the plane roared past and the shore became visible again with 'Welcome to Victoria' spelled out in gay flowers on a grassy bank; to starboard the granite legislative buildings looked down upon a marina full of yachts, ahead stood the lovely old creeper-clad Empress Hotel, and to the left of it the customs float reappeared with a figure standing on it beckoning us in. As we approached we saw that this was our friend Tom Denny. He had seen our two white masts from his hilltop home that morning and had hurried down to meet us.

*   *   *

For a day or two *Wanderer* shared a marina with float planes while we enjoyed the attractive and colourful city, which is not only the capital of Vancouver Island but of all British Columbia, with its flowers, fine buildings, well-stocked shops and museums in one of which, the Maritime Museum, Voss's *Tilikum* and Guzzwell's *Trekka* are now housed.

It was a strange coincidence that our visit should coincide with the publication of an issue of the monthly journal of the Maritime Museum carrying a picture of HMS *Condor* on the cover, and inside an account of the events leading up to her loss with all hands near Cape Flattery in a heavy winter gale in 1902, for one of Susan's many uncles, Commander Clifton Sclater RN, was her commanding officer and had been since her first commissioning. Unknown to us Susan's cousin, Jenifer Faulkner, had recently been in Victoria gathering what details she could about the disaster for an erudite article she was to write for *The Mariner's Mirror*.

Condor was a 180-foot, three masted, barque-rigged steam gunvessel of 980 tons with a crew, including officers, of 105. Her voyage out from Chatham by way of the Strait of Magellan to join the Pacific squadron, had been difficult because of her violent motion and inefficiency under either sail or steam, and there had been several cases of yellow fever on board.

After a refit at the Esquimalt base near Victoria, she was ordered to sail for Hawaii and repair Cook's grave there, then deliver mail to Pitcairn Island, after which she was to report on the labour situation in the South Sea Islands (slave trade) and look for castaways on uninhabited islands – all highly romantic, no doubt, but what an undertaking! She sailed on 2 December and was not heard of again, but wreckage from her was found along the seaward shores of Vancouver Island.

It is clear from Mrs Faulkner's research that the blame for the loss of *Condor* must be placed on the ship's designers, for the little vessel was crank: she often rolled to 25° and sometimes to 34°, the roll being aggravated by the need to carry 48 tons of reserve bunker coal and stores on the upper deck, and when a sea was shipped her high bulwarks, which were provided with freeing ports of insufficient number and size, trapped a great weight of water there. Sclater reported these and other defects of the newly-built vessel, but a Mr Moorish (assistant constructor 1st class in Admiralty) refused to sanction any modifications, denying that anything from his department could possibly be wrong.

*   *   *

It was a pale-blue, sunny day when we came towards the head of Saanich Inlet in Vancouver Island and identified the Dennys' island, low and small but graced by some splendid arbutus trees, their red trunks standing out bright against the grey of the rock. As we approached, a big Canadian flag crept to the truck of a flagstaff, and when we came in alongside the float Tom and Margaret were waiting there to take our lines and give us one of the most charming welcomes we have ever had.

Just ahead of us, and so close that the gilded tip of *Wanderer*'s bowsprit almost touched her gleaming bow, lay their ketch, *Daphne Isle*, moored all-fours in a neat little dock of her own, and one might never have guessed that she had made the 8,000-mile voyage out from England; indeed, so immaculate was she in her coats of shining paint and varnish that she might only that day have left her builder's yard. In Canada a float is what English people call a pontoon, and Americans a slip, i.e. something that rises and falls with the tide; this one must have measured 75 feet or more in length, and instead of being held in position by posts or piles, it relied entirely on hinged cantilevers holding it to the island, the whole affair having been built of timber that had washed ashore there, a bounteous supply of which litters every beach.

At the top of the gangway we were shown the workshop, a fascinating place with every tool a voyager might need and which we were encouraged to use, and hanging on the walls and beams a great accumulation of gear, fittings, and all manner of bits and pieces which might come in handy one day. A granite path, laid by Margaret, climbed to the house at the summit of the 1½-acre island. This, like the float, they had built themselves largely from driftwood; it was a proper little home, simple, and yet with all 'mod cons'; water, electricity, washing machine, and even a telephone, by means of which I was, one morning, able to make a tape recording with the BBC in London while I looked out of the wide window at the distant mountains of Saltspring Island. All these conveniences, we were given to understand, were to be used by us: 'Just feel it's yours,' said Margaret as, with her hands on our shoulders, she showed us round, and there were times when we did almost feel that, for the Dennys were not always at the island as they had a town house and other commitments.

Wanderer looked sea-stained after her 7,000-mile voyage, with rust bleeding from ports and coach-roof coamings, and varnish peeling. We felt she was no credit to us and did not improve the appearance of the island; perhaps Tom and Margaret thought so too, for they were soon on board with chipping hammers, wire brushes and an electric grinder, and set to. Rarely have I seen people work so hard and so well, and although they were older than we were they put in a full day, and we, working with them, had a struggle to keep up, for there were no tea or coffee breaks, or the smoke'o to which we were accustomed in New Zealand, but I did occasionally creep away on some pretext to light a pipe. The mess was almost indescribable, as those who have ever had any experience of working with rusty steel will well understand, but there was a powerful vacuum cleaner to tidy that up, and hot showers ashore for dirty bodies, and often in the evening there were drinks aboard *Daphne Isle*. The weather being fine the work went on uninterrupted until it was done, for once the Dennys have set their hands to a job they continue until it is brought to a satisfactory conclusion. The place came to be known among us all as 'Denny's Devil Island Shipyard'.

Meanwhile a pair of gulls which had nested on the roof of the house were rearing a couple of chicks; there was a lot of talk between them, but they did not seem to understand that they must feed their family; so, once a day Margaret reluctantly put down her wire brush and, sitting on the float between the bows of the two ships, jigged for tiddlers, usually with instant succcss, and tossed her catch up on the roof. There were other inhabitants: swift kingfishers and hoarse herons, and occasionally we saw a mink doing his slinky rounds. However, the most extraordinary sight was the multitude of jellyfish; so close-packed were they that one could not thrust a boathook into the water without damaging several, and we had to give up using the seawater pump in the heads because the jellyfish blocked up the inlet. Among this vast armada a few yellow jellyfish of the stinging kind, two feet or more in diameter, slowly pulsed along.

At last the big job on board was finished, the rust-free steel was coated with some very special epoxy which Tom insisted on using at (his) considerable expense, and was finished in white enamel. Then off we went in company with the Dennys, they in their ship and we in ours, on a late-summer cruise. I am not going to say much about it, enjoyable though it was for us, as you might get bored unless you happen to know the waters, but I would like just to whet your appetite so that perhaps one day you may decide to sail out there and try it for yourself.

Briefly the geography is like this: Vancouver Island extends in a north-west/south-east direction for 250 miles. The city of Victoria, where we entered on arrival, lies at the south-east corner. The city of Vancouver (you may well feel confused as did we at first) is on the mainland some 50 miles from Victoria, with which it is connected by ferry. The north-east side of the southern half of Vancouver Island is separated from the Canadian mainland by the Strait of Georgia. I suppose I could count on the charts the number of islands that lie in that stretch of sheltered water and tell you how many there are, but I think it will suffice to say there are a great many; some are even smaller than the Dennys' island, others, like Texada, are more than 20 miles long. This was the area that we went cruising in; it is so sheltered from the ocean that there is never any swell, but a short, steep sea can get up quickly when wind and tide are opposed.

In the South Pacific, where we had been for the past two years, we rarely bothered about the tides which amount to little there, but now our days were to be governed by them. At narrow places between the islands the tidal streams can run at up to 12 knots, and it is wise to navigate such narrows at slack water so as to avoid the whirlpools where kelp and lumber spin; but slack water may last for only a few minutes and does not always occur at the times predicted in the tide tables. In most places the water is deep right up to the shore, but many of the islands have anchorages in moderate depths, and a lot of these are snug and secure, and the Dennys, after many years of cruising in the area, knew the best and most attractive of them, which of course they proudly showed to us. They also knew where apples and blackberries abounded, and where to fish successfully for salmon.

An interesting man-made feature in the southern part of the Strait is that the Canadian/U.S.A. border runs among the islands, so that within an hour or so one can go from one country to the other. Of course one has to enter officially each time this happens, but there are sufficient ports of entry to enable this to be done with little inconvenience, except that (since our time there coincided with the school holidays, and yachts, both Canadian and American, had proliferated to such a degree) there was sometimes a queue. I recall that when on our own we visited Roche Harbour in the American island of San Juan, *Wanderer* had to take up a position in a queue with eleven other yachts, most of them high-powered motor-cruisers or sport-fishermen. There was only one berth at the customs float which we, with our ponderous vessel, felt we could berth at with some certainty of being able to get away again, yet each time we cautiously approached it one of the impatient power-yachts astern jumped the queue to shoot in and berth ahead of us; it was not until a kind bystander, realising our problem, shooed others away that we were able to get in alongside. We knew that the U.S. Agricultural Department did not like Canadian fruit or vegetables to be imported, so Susan had been careful when buying provisions to obtain only potatoes and grapefruit grown in California. Nevertheless, the young officer seized the lot because, he said, they were not stamped 'Made in the U.S.A.'. Later we found the whole pile lying on the floor in the customs office, so whatever it was the Americans were so afraid of no doubt soon spread throughout San Juan. Returning to Canada was easier, for the officer only asked if we had any U.S. beer on board, there being a brewery workers' strike on in Canada at that time, and the American beverage was in great demand.

Having for so many years done our own pilotage in strange waters with, as it were, a chart in one hand and binoculars in the other, our little cruise in company with the Dennys was something of a holiday, for although we had been lent sailing directions—including that excellent volume *Cruising Guide to the Gulf Islands* by Bill Wolferson—and all the necessary charts (Canadian charts, like those published in the U.S.A., come in a variety of sizes, and most have to be folded into four, which makes them awkward to stow and to use) we did not often have to do our own pilotage because the Dennys led us into each anchorage, usually circling round and showing us the best spot to let go in, and they guided us unerringly through all the more awkward places. Indeed, *Daphne Isle*'s pretty stern became a familiar signpost, and she was nice about it, for being of a more slippery shape than *Wanderer*, she could go faster than we could under power, and perhaps under sail though we had little opportunity to test this, and never once did she grow impatient and become a runaway pilot.

Many of the anchorages were packed with yachts, and in the smaller and more congested of them *Daphne Isle* went in first to see if there was room for both of us, and as we had been lent walkie-talkies for this trip—little black boxes which at first I regarded with suspicion but eventually came almost to enjoy— she could tell us whether or not to come in. The overcrowding was the one thing to which we never became accustomed, and next was the fact that many of the island shores were fringed with holiday homes to make landing, except below high water mark, impossible without trespassing. Much of the southern part of the Strait proved to be a holiday playground, almost a 'suburbia-by-the-sea', with mum, dad, and the kids enjoying themselves in high-speed runabouts which dragged steep waves astern, and water-skiers doing their thing. There were even some American power-yachts that had engines running all through the night, presumably to keep deep freeze chambers cold to preserve the salmon they had caught and were going to take home, a procedure about which the Canadians had strong feelings. Some islands had marine parks, which were clean and well kept, and usually had easy and attractive trails to walk; each had a float for visitors, or moorings (free), heads, water, refuse containers and picnic tables, and sometimes at the entrance to a harbour one would see a big notice-board with Pirate's Cove, or whatever, painted boldly upon it as though to reassure the visitor that he or she had come to the right place.

We went north through Dodd Narrows (there at springs a nine knot stream runs through the passage which is only half a cable wide), left to port one of the enormous smoke-belching paper mills which are a conspicuous feature of these parts, and to which great rafts (or booms) of logs are towed from the logging camps by diminutive tugs. Often logs break adrift from these rafts, and occasionally an entire raft gets broken up in heavy weather, so floating logs up to 70 feet long and weighing many tons may be encountered anywhere. When a log becomes waterlogged it may assume an upright position (hemlock is particularly prone to this) and float with its top awash or just submerged; it is then known as a dead-head, and is a serious navigational hazard. To minimise the risk of striking one, yachts rarely move after nightfall, but even in daylight a dead-head is hard to see. Occasionally a bird perched on it will show its position, but at the time of our visit there was a move afoot to provide the numerous motor launches and speed boats which use these waters with flags on metal sticks, a flag to be planted firmly on any dead-head seen. This had the additional merit of providing motorboats with something worthwhile to do instead of rushing aimlessly around.

Having left the town of Nanaimo astern, we came into more remote and austere waters which were not so heavily populated; we crossed the Strait of Georgia diagonally, and in time made our way up through Surge Narrows (11 to 12 knot stream there at springs), where we passed so close to a submerged rock that we could have touched it with an oar, and wriggled in to a wild and lonely anchorage among the Octopus Islands. It rained while we were there, indeed it rained for most of our cruise, but we were expecting that, and I do believe this Canadian scenery looks best, perhaps I should have said it looks more as one expects it to look, in the rain with the mountains wreathed mysteriously in mist or cloud, and the firs and pines all a-drip, while the still, dark water shows little pock-marks where the raindrops fall. White smoke with the pleasant aroma of burning wood rose vertically from the chimney of our consort, in whose cosy saloon we were invited to dine that evening, not on freshly-caught salmon, for Margaret knew I did not appreciate fish, but on a splendid roast of beef.

We had heard of Desolation Sound, a name to make the blood tingle or run chill according to one's mood. Vancouver, the first white man to explore those waters, which he did in 1792, gave it that name, and it is clear from his writings that he thought little of it. Yet, when seen in the sunshine as we chanced to see it, it is breathtaking: the blue mountains topped with snow, the clean air dry and cool, the rocks pink and golden, the silence and the space immeasurable. Desolation Sound is blessed with some of the snuggest little harbours imaginable, particularly those in Cortes Island, and these we explored by dinghy—not in our dinghy, which being only 7½ feet long is no fun to row, but in Tom's fine longboat, which was carried in davits across *Daphne Isle*'s stern. With two of us rowing she provided water transport of the sort which today has almost been forgotten, the long oars leaving widely spaced puddles, the boat running easily and true between the measured strokes. In the rain as well the sight of us all in yellow oilskins sometimes created a stir at an anchorage, for in these days of inflatables and outboards few people row for pleasure. As we slipped silently along we were sometimes asked if we were going far, or if we would like a tow; our reply that we were just out for fun raised a surprised smile or a doubtful shake of the head. There were many things about *Daphne Isle* that took our fancy, but above all Susan and I did envy her that long dinghy. We in *Wanderer* had no suitable place in which to carry such a boat, and stern davits were ruled out for us by our need for a wind-vane steering gear.

The cruise in company lasted for three weeks; the passages between one anchorage and another varied in distance from one to 40 miles, and sometimes we visited more than one place in a day. The total distance made good was 340 miles, but because of the almost continuous calm we managed to sail only 25 of those miles. It had been a memorable experience, but we were all happy to return to Denny's Devil Island Shipyard, where Tom and Margaret at once undertook some further big maintenance jobs for us; the final and perhaps the most satisfying one was done on the last fine day of autumn, when the four of us managed to rub down all the brightwork and get a coat of varnish on in time to harden before the damp night set in.

Thereafter, shortening days and increasing rain called a halt to any further operations. The jellyfish went to deeper water, the arbutus trees erupted in a blaze of scarlet berries, and sadly the fallen maple leaves came slowly drifting by. It was time for us to light the cabin stove and seek our winter quarters.

*   *   *

The Dickinsons in *Kapduva* were leaving for the South Pacific, and they arranged for us to take over their berth at Van Isle

Marina which was to be run by their sons in their absence. The marina welcomed live-aboards, realising that they provide the best form of security–the light shining out of the porthole, the murmur of voices, the smell of cooking, smoke from the chimney, may well cause intruders to think again. It was a big marina and our berth in front of the Dickinson house was in the best part of it, well sheltered from most winds by trees and rows of brightly painted floating boatsheds in which power yachts lay protected from the weather.

Our friends assured us that Vancouver Island winters are never severe, but we felt apprehensive when we learnt that some of them were planning to fly away to Mexico or Hawaii for a few months. Others who remained told us when the winter was over that they had not known one quite so severe for a long time. We soon had to abandon the sleeping cabin which, being separated from the rest of the accommodation by the centre cockpit and engine room, became much too cold, and we slept instead in the saloon with the heating stove going continuously day and night, and usually managed to keep just warm enough.

We put to sea only once that winter to give a talk and slide show, organised by the Thermopylae Club in Victoria, and we berthed at the marina overlooked by the Parliament buildings in the heart of the city, where we had to put money in a meter every twelve hours just as though we were parking a car. A bitter north-easter whistled through the streets and across the harbour, and in the evening as we made our way to the theatre where a large and enthusiastic audience had gathered, the gale was driving before it a flurry of snow; next morning the sea water in which our ship lay was thinly coated with ice. We had a lot of visitors, and each time the companionway was opened to let them below all the heat was sucked out and time was needed for it to build up again. So we were glad to get back to our cozy winter quarters, unbend the sails, double up our lines, and rig a small awning to keep the rain and snow out of the cockpit.

At Christmas time there were 15°F (8°C) of frost on deck, two of our hatches became frozen up, as did the marina's water supply together with its heads and washing machines, and remained so for several weeks. Friends brought us water from their homes in bottles and other containers, for although our tanks and pipes, which were below the waterline, did not freeze we were getting low on water because we had emptied one tank to ensure that when we took the ground and sewed a little on the coming minus tides, which were due to occur in the night, we would list the right way against the pontoon and not lean on our neighbour. The lowest of those tides coincided with a southeast gale which roared in the trees and lifted and dropped with metallic crashes some of the boathouse roofs. The ship listed more than before, and we on deck were hard put to it to keep fenders in place as the float against which we leant creaked and dropped lower and lower. The heater blew out and by dawn the cabin temperature was well below freezing. We saw little of our fellow marina inhabitants, for most went away all day to various jobs, but sometimes in the dark on my early morning walks I met one or two trying to start their reluctant snow-dusted cars as I crossed the parking lot, and we briefly exchanged greetings. But in spite of the cold we enjoyed our winter in British Columbia, for we were busy and we experienced much kindness and hospitality from many families living in the neighbourhood.

Many years ago when Adlard Coles owned and edited *The Yachtsman* (then the oldest yachting magazine in the world, but now, I believe, defunct) and I was working for him, a new typist, Catherine Webb, was engaged. After a few months Adlard wanted to get rid of her, but I said he should not do that for she was an attractive girl, was clearly doing her best, and probably needed the money; so she stayed on. Now she was happily married to Pip Holmes, who as well as running the family real estate business in Victoria was *aide-de-camp* to the Lieutenant Governor of British Columbia. Pip and Catherine were most hospitable, and among other events devised for our pleasure invited us to their lovely home to dine with His Excellency and Mrs Bell-Irving, people to whom we took an instant liking. Also present were Admiral Martin, Commander in Chief for the Pacific Coast, and his wife.

The Admiral took Susan and me severely to task when he learnt that we did not carry ship/shore radio; indeed he went so far as to suggest that this was irresponsible and he returned to the matter again and again.

Mrs Bell-Irving took our side. 'I quite understand their desire for privacy,' she said. 'Why should they have to bother with a telephone if they don't want one?'

'How,' the Admiral returned, 'would they be able to let us know if an aircraft ditched beside them?'

'They wouldn't need to,' put in Catherine with a smile, 'I'm sure they would go to the rescue. Eric has done something of the sort before, you know.'

It was good to see the girl to whom I used to dictate my letters now an elegant and well-established hostess, so competently running her gracious home, and so ready to spring to the defence of her old friends in the face of big naval guns.

*   *   *

In the spring we got hauled out at Canoe Cove and, because of the peculiarities of British Columbia tides, this had to be done at one o'clock in the morning. Using any slip for the first time is worrying even though one may have confidence in the person running it, but to do so in the dark with an unknown man in charge is nerve racking. Considering the time of day, it was surprising to find about a dozen people standing on the side platforms of the cradle as we moved into it, and several of them shouted conflicting suggestions and advice which must have confused the operator, for he drove wedges in between the arms of the cradle and our bottom and started his winch before the ship had settled on her keel, thus putting great pressure on small areas of the plating. Twice he did this, and eventually I had to give orders myself: 'Lower us back into the water; take out the wedges; now haul until we are sitting firmly on our keel, and only then put in the wedges'.

Some friends had come along to help us do the work, and as soon as we were fully out of the water they illuminated our bottom with the headlights of their cars while they scrubbed off the slime and weed. Soon after daylight a young couple who had been assisting in the night turned up again to help us paint the bottom, and with their aid we got two coats of anti-fouling on it. When the job was finished we gave them a little present, but after they had left I found it tucked neatly into one of my shoes.

The last time we had hauled out was in New Zealand before starting the voyage, and on that occasion we had discovered several tiny holes in the plating in way of the chain locker. Apparently a hair crack had opened between the plating and the cement with which the builders had made level the bottom of the locker, and water from the chain as it was hove in had entered there and rusted the plating through from the inside. We had the holes welded. Now we found some fresh holes in the same area, but as getting them welded would have caused delay, and the slip having been booked for another vessel, we plugged them with some quick-setting filler. The matter was not serious, but we knew that at some future date the cement, which should never have been put there, would have to be chipped away and the plating renewed.

Of course we had to be launched in the dark, but that was no problem. We returned to our marina berth for a few days to service the wind-vane steering gear, which had grown stiff in its nylon joints over the long, wet winter, and to make our farewells to the many who had befriended us. Towards the end of April we moved to the Royal Victoria Yacht club to get our out-of-bond stores, dear Margaret Denny made a special journey from her home to cut Susan's hair on the lawn, we obtained our outward clearance and with sadness left British Columbia.

There was no breath of wind that day as we motored down Juan de Fuca Strait with sea and sky like pewter, passing outside Race Rocks this time and dipping our largest ensign to the Andersons. There would have been little point in going to sea in such weather, so once again we made use of the excellent anchorage in Neah Bay near Cape Flattery to wait for some wind, and took the opportunity to obtain a U.S. cruising permit, for we intended to call in at some California ports on our way back to New Zealand. That civilised document permits a foreign yacht to go where she pleases in U.S. waters for a period of six months without further formality; it costs nothing and when it expires can usually be renewed. Some other countries, such as Fiji, which make such a fuss about visiting yachts, would do well to follow this example. As on other occasions on the American coast we found the official quick and courteous, and he did not even enquire if we had out-of-bond stores on board. It was just as well that we did stop at Neah Bay, for after a day of heavy rain, through which the foghorns hooted dismally, a southerly gale blew and fifty salmon trollers, looking very smart in their coats of spring paint, came into the anchorage for shelter.

The delay made us decide not to stop at San Francisco, as originally planned, so when we did get away we stood out to sea for 60 miles to get clear of the shipping lanes and the inshore fog, and then for the next 800 miles kept parallel to the coast. The wind came from the north-west and worked itself up to gale force; we ran before it, and on one occasion made a day's run of 161 miles under the close-reefed main alone, with the rejuvenated vane gear doing all the steering. We cleared the State of Washington in one day, Oregon in two, and on the fourth were in Californian waters. Towards the end the wind fell light, and it died right away as we closed with the land and, under power, rounded Point Conception, which Californian yachtsmen regard as their local Cape Horn because of the difficulty of doubling it when northbound against the prevailing north-west wind and in the fog which is common there. Seven days out of Neah Bay, and with 1,000 miles astern of us, we anchored outside the kelp on the east side of Santa Rosa Island, where the cattle ranch homestead – the only dwelling on that 15-mile-long island – stood at the edge of the cliffs, and enjoyed a night of undisturbed sleep.

It was still calm and grey in the morning when we got our anchor and motored on towards San Diego, 170 miles distant, where mail and friends awaited us, and the following forenoon, in poor visibility, we made a landfall. On the port bow loomed a headland and across our bows spread a low sandy shore with high-rise buildings behind it. This, we thought, was the beach fronting San Diego Bay, so the headland should have been Point Loma at the entrance to San Diego Harbour. We altered course toward it, but as it grew more distinct we could see no lighthouse nor any of the buoys marking the entrance channel, and turned away, perplexed. We had not long to wait for noon, by which time the horizon to the south had cleared and the overcast had thinned enough to permit me to get a noon latitude sight which showed we were 10 miles north of where we thought we were. The features were similar: a headland (La Jolla) and a sand beach (Mission Bay), and it drove home once again a lesson I thought I had learnt many years ago—never jump to conclusions when making a landfall just because the features you are expecting to see appear to fall into place. On the clanging bell-buoy at the entrance we found a seal sleeping, apparently preferring that noisy resting place to the silent ones nearby, and it was late afternoon when we came to the yacht harbour inside Shelter Island (which was made from spoil dredged from the channel, and is now almost overrun with marinas, hotels and restaurants), and berthed at the San Diego Yacht Club's guest dock.

Nine years had passed since we had spent a 12-month period there while I recovered from an injury sustained on the coast of Mexico, so we had plenty of friends who seemed to have changed little and, as before, almost overwhelmed us with kindness. One couple, for example, had us to dine the evening after our arrival and then took us to the opera where, I am ashamed to say, I slept through most of *Pagliacci* (which followed *Cavalleria Rusticana*) for I was still weary after the passage. They also lent us one of their fleet of five cars, an enormous gas-guzzling Chevy station-wagon with brimming tank, to help us with our shopping; and we shopped in a big way, mostly for *Wanderer* who had by now got through all the good things we had bought for her there on the earlier visit. After the first three days the club charged the visiting yacht about U.S. $10 a day; but as she was given a pontoon berth with freshwater supply, security and electricity (if she could make use of it), and we had the run of a fine club house with restaurant, bar, swimming pool and showers, the charge was not excessive and was less than at some of the commercial marinas in that harbour.

We remained among the immaculate and glistening marina-based fleet for only twelve days because we wanted to get down to about five degrees north before the middle of June, after which there is some risk of tropical revolving storms in the eastern part of the ocean north of that latitude. As very few storm tracks are shown on the pilot charts it may be considered that we were a bit too apprehensive; but since the advent of meteorological satellites a lot more tropical storms have been reported than in earlier days when, because of the lack of shipping in that wide and lonely area, many may have formed and passed unnoticed.

In a calm we motored seaward to look for the 24-knot north-wester which was reported to be blowing, but there was no wind under the leaden sky, and for the next 11 days conditions remained much the same. We got sufficient glimpses of the woolly sun through the murk for navigational purposes, but in all that time we saw no stars. We made what use we could of the occasional light airs, usually under genoa, mizzen staysail, or running sail, or a combination, for the heavier working sails could not hold their wind as we rolled in the persistent north-west swell. We were reluctant to use fuel which we would probably want later among the islands and reefs of the South Pacific, and for battery-charging. However, with hurricanes much in mind we felt we should press on under power in the long-lasting calms, and at slow and economical speed did so for some 500 miles in those first 11 days.

At 48 minutes past every hour the U.S. radio station WWVH, which broadcasts time continuously on 2.5, 5, 10 and 15 MHz, gives brief weather warnings for the Pacific. Listening to these throughout the month-long passage, we learnt that every single day there was dense fog north of 40°N; of course this did not concern us now, but it confirmed our belief that the northern part of this ocean is a gloomy place. Of immediate interest, however, was the report of an early tropical storm given the name Andreas, and day by day we followed her progress, noting with relief that she kept near the Mexican coast and finally turned inland. We heard later, with rather smug feelings, of another storm called Bianca which crossed our track only a week after we had passed that way.

From the weather point of view we might perhaps have done better to have gone by way of Hawaii, but that would have increased the total distance to Tahiti (the island for which we were bound, by about 1,000 miles, and since the pilot chart for June indicated that we should reach the region of the north-east trade wind just as directly by keeping to the rhumb line, that was the course we took; it is, incidentally, almost identical to the great circle course. We expected to find the trade in about 25°N, but had to go a lot further south than that before we felt the first long-awaited breath of it. Then at last the sky cleared as though some giant, with one broad sweep, had carried the cloud cover away, and at 19°N Susan was able to check our latitude with an observation of Polaris in the middle of the night, so brilliantly was the northern horizon illuminated by the full moon. Once we had reached it the trade wind never faltered, and a few degrees north of the equator, where we expected to have to pass through the doldrum belt, we found no doldrums; the north-east wind just shifted round to a little south of east and continued to blow. So the statement in the *Pilot*, which I had noted on the voyage north, had on this occasion proved its veracity.

Had we kept exactly to the rhumb line we would have crossed the equator in 140°W, but three vigias lie in that neighbourhood: 'Discoloured water' and two lots of 'Breakers reported'. The information about these possible dangers given in the *Pilot* and its supplement is vague, so we passed a degree to the west of them. This was our ninth crossing of the equator, so except for an extra tot in the evening there were no celebrations on board.

There was plenty of weight in the wind thereafter, and for a whole week (in which we made good nearly 1,000) we had reefs in the main and mizzen, and forward with the staysail we could comfortably carry only the small jib. We detected little sign of any current, and in the forenoon of our 28th day at sea we sighted at a distance of about 10 miles the tops of the palms on Mataiva, the westernmost atoll of the Tuamotu Archipelago. This was a surprise, for according to the latest determinations Mataiva lies five miles east of its charted position (which we had been steering to clear) and should therefore have been out of sight. Nevertheless it was good to see that fringe of green on the horizon after so long a time away from land.

The following day we took our navigation even more seriously than usual; I got a forenoon, a noon, and an afternoon observation of the sun, and at evening dusk Susan confirmed my carried-forward position with a round of star sights. The reason for such unusual activity was that during the night we would be passing the low atoll of Tetiaroa, which lies in the northern approach to Tahiti and has claimed its share of wrecks. We knew that the current runs strongly to the west there. John Evans in *Stortebecker III* had stopped and secured to a ruined jetty on the atoll's southern shore, and he reported that the west-flowing current was constant and strong enough to tail his yacht away from the jetty throughout the several days he remained. More recently the maxi ocean racer *Condor of Bermuda*, shortly after setting out from Tahiti on a passage towards Hawaii, stranded by night on the southern shore of the atoll and was severely damaged; but successful efforts at salvage were made, and she was shipped back to New Zealand for rebuilding.

The island was owned by a film star and is visited by tourists from Tahiti, so one might have thought that someone would have established a light on it; but nobody had. The night turned particularly dark, the wind increased to 35 knots (on deck) and the sea was rough. Anxious hours passed until we reckoned by the log reading that we were safely past the danger, which we left up-wind and (we hoped) up-current; then hardening in the sheets we came on the wind and plunged on toward Tahiti. Presently the loom in the sky of the lights of Papeete appeared, but feeling a little stetched at the end of our 30-day passage, during which we had come 3,600 miles, we were disinclined to submit ourselves to the crowded harbour and the port officials until we had rested; so we hove-to for the remainder of the night, and at dawn let draw and hurried towards the mountains spires of Moorea. There we shot through the pass, where the sea was breaking heavily and noisily on either hand, into what seemed like another world, a place of luxurious vegetation, smooth water, and little wind; the smell of flowers and wood smoke drifted out to us along with muted sounds from the land as we crept to a mountain-girt anchorage, let go, and spread the awning.

On the passage we had seen very little wildlife once the California coast had been left astern, and we sighted only four vessels. One was a very large fisherman ablaze with lights and apparently riding to a net, the ends of which were marked by light-buoys five miles apart–no wonder the oceans are becoming so empty of life. The second was a tanker, bound, we concluded, from Panama to Hawaii. The third was a mystery. She came swooping over the swell one night when we were near the equator to blind us with a searchlight, and close off our port side, still with her light trained on us, kept station for perhaps 10 minutes. Our ship must have presented a stirring sight as she roared along, well heeled under her tan sails, flinging her bow wave high, her port light a splash of vivid scarlet; but at the time we were more concerned with the possibility of being hijacked, though that seemed unlikely in an area so far from land, and were much relieved when our unwelcome visitor extinguished her light and turned away. The fourth vessel went unidentified as she was some distance off and vanished in a rain squall.

Like all other foreign yachts we had to post a bond on arrival at Papeete. For British and other Europeans this was the equivalent of U.S. $1,000 for each person on board, and for Australian, New Zealand and U.S. yachts the bond was $500 per person. The money was refunded at the final port of departure in that group of French islands, provided there was a bank there and it had sufficient cash. Meanwhile, if the French invested it they must have been doing pretty well with perhaps 150 overseas yachts among their islands with, say, an average of four people in each. We remained only for two days at the noisy waterfront, and then returned to Moorea to enjoy a week's walking, swimming and meeting the other voyagers at that spectacular island which is one of our favourites.

It was at Moorea that we experienced for the first time a nuisance which is becoming increasingly common in anchorages shared with yachts which use ship/shore radio. When the owners are transmitting they can cause so much interference on all of the short-wave bands that their neighbours and people ashore cannot listen to the B.B.C., A.B.C., N.Z.B.C., etc. I am told that this is because the transmitters are defective (something to do with filters?) and I suggest that the amateur operators might regard as a silent period the 20 minutes starting at each hour, for it is then that the news is broadcast by most national stations—we at the time wanted to hear about the Fastnet race, but could not.

On this occasion we did not much enjoy cruising among the Society Islands, for there was no wind, yet a steep and confused sea was running. In addition, of course, air transport had brought them within easy reach of the tourist, and tourism appears to have a bad effect on island communities. For example, at Bora Bora (advertised as the most beautiful island in the world) which has several hotels and a yacht club, we found the islanders downright surly, not least the woman at the bank whose job it was to refund our bond. Yet at Tahaa, where there was no hotel and probably no air service, and where few yachts called, we found the villagers at Hamene Bay cheerful and busy with their proper island affairs.

Our intention on leaving Bora Bora was to sail direct to Fiji, and for the first four days we had a steady trade wind and good sailing. But then the wind fell light and variable, the glass began to fall, ominous blue-black clouds massed to the westward and rapidly advanced upon us bringing rain. We heeded the warnings and reduced sail, and it was as well that we did so, for at dusk a squall of great violence sprang at us. The surface of the sea was white with low-driven spume, a remarkable sight under the heavy black sky, and the roaring wind and the torrential rain made it difficult for us to breathe or communicate as we dragged down and secured the staysail and wound the reefing handle until the mainsail was only a quarter of its full area. While I was doing this my bare feet trod with horrified surprise upon a long, sodden, hairy creature; it proved to be a length of baggy-wrinkle torn from aloft by the wind. We lashed the helm down and left the ship hove-to throughout the night, which was punctuated by similar storm-force squalls. When lying hove-to or a-hull we liked to hinge the servo blade of the vane gear up out of the water to save it from the considerable lateral strains otherwise imposed, and it was while this was being done that a sea slammed the blade to leeward, something broke, and the bevel wheels became disengaged. Inaccessibility and the constant motion prevented any attempt to effect repairs at sea, or even to discover exactly what was wrong; that would have to wait until we could launch the dinghy in a quiet anchorage, so we decided to put in at one of the Tonga Islands. But Vava'u, the nearest of them, lay all of 500 miles away, and the weather remained bad with squalls and calms for the next six days. Sometimes our progress was so poor that it scarcely seemed worthwhile to stay out steering in the almost continuous rain, and we spent several nights lying a-hull to save the sails from slatting and to get some rest—indeed, after 50,000 miles under the capable control of the Aries vane gear we had grown out of the habit of steering and quickly became bored.

As on earlier visits we found Vava'u unspoilt, and its people dignified and unsophisticated. One day when we were on the wharf photographing inter-island travel de luxe à la Tonga, a young woman passenger stepped ashore from the battered old trader to ask if we would take a picture of her and her sister; in some other islands a fee would have been demanded had the request come from us. We gained the impression that the people were poor, though obviously not ill-fed; such few provisions as were available were cheap, and we found that the baker still made some of the best crusty bread in the South Pacific.

A windless day enabled us to investigate the trouble with the vane gear from the dinghy, and we discovered that an end tooth had been broken off the lower bevel gear. We were able to get the gear to work again by re-engaging the bevel wheels and restricting the swing of the vane by lengthening its stops with bits of plastic hose, and we hoped that a letter to the maker would get a replacement part to us at Suva in Fiji.

Since leaving Tahiti we had been unfortunate with the weather, and on the passage to Suva we had nothing but calms and light headwinds; indeed throughout the months of July and August, when at sea, we experienced no more than four days of proper trade wind sailing.

Busy, noisy, down-at-heels Suva used to be our favourite island town, bursting with people, traffic, battered little trading vessels and fishing craft. There were forty overseas yachts at anchor off the Royal Suva Yacht Club, which is handy for the town, and a similar number off the Tradewinds Hotel. We preferred to spend most of our time in the cleaner, quieter anchorage by Mosquito Island, which only a few others used— notably those who wished to scrub and paint their bottoms, for the tiny island has the only sand beach for miles around. Each day during the school holidays, however, the beach was alive with mop-headed children with big eyes and flashing smiles playing and bathing; pandemonium reigned, but never did we hear a cross word or a cry of fright or pain. Other visitors to our retreat were slender sea-snakes, handsome in their silver, black-ringed skins; they spent many hours cruising along our waterline investigating the secret scupper outlets and other holes; it is said that their venom is deadly but they are not of a belligerent nature.

However, we were so abominably treated by a racist party of four port officials (one Fijian and three Indian) that we will never call at Suva again. These men boarded us from the hotel launch the day before we left, and after we had obtained our clearance. They took the clearance and our passports from us, though we had done nothing wrong, and for 20 minutes or so taunted and abused us, their pleasure clearly being to bait the British.

We left next day in a state almost bordering on shock, and with a fresh breeze on the beam sailed swiftly down Kandavu Passage to take our departure for New Zealand from Cape Washington's brilliant light. Again, and you must be getting almost as tired of this as we were, we had poor sailing conditions which started the next night with a tremendous electric storm, when each great clap of thunder almost coincided with the lightning flash, and each flash was so vivid that objects it had revealed remained imprinted on the retinas of our eyes long after. Then we had a headwind, and when this reached Force 7 we jogged along at about 1½ knots under the reefed mainsail alone, for to make better progress in such conditions was scarcely worth the wear and tear on the gear and ourselves, and we continued like that for 80 hours. The distance from Suva to the Bay of Islands is about 1,100 miles, and the trip took 13 days.

We closed with the land a little anxiously by night in heavy rain, seeing nothing, but dawn showed our landfall to be a good one; to starboard lay the low humps of the Cavalli Islands, and on the port bow stood the familiar silhouette of Cape Brett. In absolute calm we gently motored into the bay, sea and sky all pewter just as they had been the day we left British Columbia. The Ninepin, Fraser Rock, and the little town of Russell slipped by, and in the afternoon we went alongside the wharf at Opua (our base) where friends were standing by to take our lines. Milk, bread, wine and a copy of *The Herald* were handed down while we waited for the officers from Customs and Agriculture to come, and when they arrived they could not have been more considerate; of course they took our egg shells away but let us keep the insides, so we had an enormous omelette that evening, and they declined to show any interest in the few bottles of spirits remaining or in a rather expensive radio receiver we had bought in America. We just had time to collect a big pile of mail before the post office closed, then crossed the river to pick up the mooring we had dropped 18 months before to visit Canada, one of the most worthwhile and memorable trips that we had ever made.

PART II
Wanderer V

We had grown fond of the handsome ship which had served as our comfortably spacious floating home and workshop for the past twelve years and had carried us safely some 77,000 miles, but as she and we grew older we were finding that maintenance was taking too much of our time, and it was dirty, unrewarding work that we did not enjoy. Then there was that decaying chain locker to be attended to; in addition, one of the standpipes was crumbling due to galvanic action where a brass sea-cock was fitted (we wondered about the condition of the other nine), and the steel cockpit sole was in such bad shape that it needed renewing.

Out in the open ocean, smashing her 125 miles a day close-reaching through the broad band of a trade wind area or running before a gale in higher latitudes, carrying us and all our possessions to some faraway place, she was near perfect for the purpose and filled us with confidence and admiration. But with a displacement of 22 tons she asked for a larger or more agile crew if the best was to be had from her, especially in coastal waters. We agreed that the time had come to replace her with something smaller, simpler, and less demanding in upkeep as well as being easier and more fun for the pair of us to sail.

Today there are hundreds of well-proved stock boats built of glass-reinforced plastics with, presumably, most of the bugs already eradicated, and a sensible person would, no doubt, choose one of these; but we wanted the replacement to be pleasing to our eyes and have some character of her own, and, if possible, be built of wood. We did not consider buying a yacht abroad and importing her into New Zealand, which we wished to continue using as our base, because of the high duty. Taking a look at some of the yachts on the second-hand market we were not impressed with what we saw even at prices we could not possibly afford, for most were arranged below to fulfil the weekend cottage concept, having a large number of sleeping berths and much room given up to shower stalls and refrigeration chambers, but with little stowage space for sails and personal belongings.

We believed that to have something built to meet our needs would be too costly, and did not seriously consider the matter until one evening when we had been invited to dine with our friends Alan and Debbie Orams in their waterside home. Alan had been building boats most of his life and had designed a number of attractive ones; until his recent retirement he had been running his own boatbuilding yard.

He and Debbie gave our problem their thoughtful attention, and concluded that the only way we were likely to get the kind of vessel we thought we wanted would be to have her built in New Zealand, and that if kept simple she need cost little more than we might reasonably expect to get when we sold our larger vessel, yet she could still be a floating home, with a character of her own, incorporating most of our requirements, and be capable of making ocean voyages.

While we were digesting this Alan left the room and returned with a half model he had made of one of his designs. I saw as I took it from him that this was something very fine, a quite enchanting thing. There was plenty of straight keel, ample beam, a steeply raked sternpost and broad transom with a touch of Herreshoff about it, and an exciting stem and springy sheer of which the late Jack Laurent Giles might have approved. Susan and I were intrigued by it as we examined it from every angle, running our fingers along the sweet lines, until we saw that Debbie, who had prepared dinner, was growing restive, so we put it aside while we ate.

Having known Claud Worth, Conor O'Brien, Harrison Butler, Philip Allen, William Robinson, Irving Johnson and Carl Moesly, to name only a few, I was well aware that many a proper cruising man eventually designs for himself the kind of yacht that has evolved in his mind over many years, and then has her built. Susan and I, too, believed we knew what we wanted, but as I had not the skill to put this down on paper I needed help from one who could, and was fortunate to find that not only had Alan an eye for curves that satisfied me but he even agreed with some of my ideas.

I asked what a yacht, similar to the model and about 38 feet long, would normally be built of.

'Kauri, of course,' said Alan, 'three skins of it on a laminated backbone. Deck and coachroof could be of plywood to keep down weight and cost.'

Kauri was New Zealand's most favoured boatbuilding timber, but had grown scarce because early settlers had wantonly felled whole forests of the tall, straight trees and used the wood for mundane purposes such as building houses, and they did not replant.

I believe it was the thought of wood construction that finally decided us to go ahead with this (crazy?) project. Both of us are old-fashioned and, perhaps because we understand it best, regard good wood as the most trustworthy boatbuilding material. We knew it to be rewarding to work, pleasant to look at, to smell and to feel, that it provides an aura of coziness and warmth and, compared with steel, is easy and satisfying to maintain. If worm and rain are kept out, which is easily done by sheathing with epoxy and dynel, and plenty of fresh air is let in, it will last for a very long time. *Wanderer II* and *Wanderer III* were both of wood construction, the former planked with pitchpine, the latter with iroko, and both were still alive and well. *Wanderer III* had recently completed her third circumnavigation of the world in the capable and loving hands of her German owner, Giselher Ahlers; she was 28 years old, and her predecessor 15 years older than that.

It may be wondered why we should favour a long keel, transom stern and outboard rudder. This was partly because a transom is easier and therefore cheaper to build than is a counter with its rudder trunk, and steering can be done by tiller instead of wheel, and we wanted to enjoy again the thrilling little tremble of a tiller when a boat is going well. We believed that a longish keel would give better directional stability than the fin and skeg configuration. Certainly a rudder hung on the sternpost with its bottom pintle on the keel is the strongest, simplest and least troublesome of all arrangements. A long keel also makes hauling out or drying out safe and easy. Of course the wetted area is greater, though the raked sternpost would reduce this to some extent. I did wonder if that 40 degree rake would prove to be excessive, for the more nearly vertical a rudder is the more efficient it becomes; but I was reluctant to ask the expert to make major alterations to his creation unless I was convinced they were essential. I did, however, draw his attention to the fact that we would be carrying some heavy items far aft: the engine together with 60 gallons of fuel, batteries, two 20-lb gas bottles and 40 gallons of water, and I believe he allowed for this by filling out the after ends of the waterlines a little. As an experienced boatbuilder he also made some modifications to the body plan to reduce or eliminate reverse curves at the garboards, thus making construction a little easier. Alan declined the architect's fee, which of course we offered, and most generously made us a present of the design.

The amended drawing showed the following statistics:

LOA 39½ feet
LWL 33½ feet
Beam, extreme 12¼ feet
Beam at LWL 11¼ feet
Draught 5¼ feet
Displacement 11 tons
Ballast keel 3¾ tons

The beam might seem excessive, but I recall that Carleton Mitchell's famous *Finisterre* was so beamy that she shocked some knowledgeable people, yet she proved to be one of the most successful yachts of her day both as a cruiser and ocean racer, and when Carleton was living aboard she carried much weight, including a set of winter moorings.

On a drawing showing some of the more important details of construction Alan marked where, with our desired amidships headroom of six feet, the edges of the cabin sole would be, and with that to work on Susan and I could now organise and draw the accommodation plan as well as the deck layout, for these

The steel ketch *Wanderer IV* – our home for thirteen years.

In Robinson Cove, Moorea.

Prideaux Haven in Desolation Sound.

Wanderer V was built upside down in typical New Zealand fashion. Here stringers are ready to accept the three skins of diagonal planking.

Turnover – almost as exciting as the launching.

The saloon looking forward. The painting recessed among the books is a David Cobb of *Wanderer III*, and the chart on the door shows our various voyages.

ABOVE LEFT Looking aft from the sleeping cabin. Companionway steps hinge up to give access to the space under the bridge deck.

ABOVE RIGHT Saloon and sleeping cabin.

The two ships shared a marina berth while we transhipped our belongings from the big one on the right to her smaller successor.

were to be entirely our responsibility. But before going further we needed to find a yard that could and would build our ship within a reasonable time.

New Zealand used to have many small and a few large boatbuilding yards where excellent work in wood was done, but since the short-sighted government had imposed a 20% tax on all new yachts and their gear, many of the yards had been forced to close and their shipwrights to seek employment in more enlightened Australia where there was no such tax. However, Orams Marine at Whangarei, Alan's old yard but with which he now had no connection, was still in business. It was well known to us, for we had often slipped there to paint the bottom, and the yard had done some little jobs for us from time to time. We also knew Ray Roberts, the new owner, and some of the people working for him; if he would build for us we felt we could scarcely be in better hands. With a little persuasion from Alan, Ray agreed to fit us into his programme and promised to have Job 40 ready for us by Christmas in about 13 months' time.

Having had two yachts built in England and one in Holland, where a price was quoted, a contract signed and payment made at stipulated stages of construction, we thought our arrangement with Ray was somewhat casual. He gave us a rough idea of what the final cost *might* be, but warned that an anticipated rise in shipwrights' wages could quickly alter this (it soon did) as also would any increase in the cost of materials or fittings. But to minimise the latter risk he at once started buying wood, glue, fastenings, lead, engine, compass, winches, ground tackle and the hundreds of other things needed, and each month we paid him for everything he had bought and for labour. I was not at all clear on the matter, but apparently we were covered against losing all in the event of fire or the yard going bankrupt, though we signed nothing at all except cheques. It seemed an odd way of doing business, and my legal liminary father was probably restless in his grave, but it proved to be entirely satisfactory.

In typical New Zealand fashion the hull was to be of three skins laid diagonally, each stapled and glued to the next, on a framework of closely placed fore-and-aft stringers. This would make such a strong walnut that only five frames would be needed, and they together with stem and keel would be laminated. Everything except the deck and joinery was to be of kauri and Ray had plenty of that timber suitable for most of the job but he needed some longer pieces of the best heart kauri for keel laminations, sternpost and deck beams, and this was not easy to come by.

However, Dick McIlvride, who owned our mooring and the property off which it lay, had laid in a stock of timber some years before for a yacht he intended to build for himself, and now, finding he had more than he needed, he sold four 25-foot balks of heart kauri to us. Each weighed 500 lb, and somehow they had to be moved out of his shed and loaded on his small barge for transport across the Waikare River to the road, where a truck with a forklift would pick them up and take them to the yard 40 miles away. Susan and I now have a better understanding of how the Pyramids were built, for apart from his own strong arms the only tools Dick used were some rollers, a few wedges and a lever. Without much fuss or apparent effort each balk silently emerged through the doorway and on to the waiting barge, almost as though self-propelled. Dick secured his outboard dinghy alongside and manoeuvred the barge across the river. The truck had not arrived, but that did not bother him, and with some rope he had thoughtfully brought along he parbuckled the balks up the bank and stacked them beside the road.

*   *   *

At the suggestion of a thoughtful customs officer who may have known what was about to happen, we had imported *Wanderer IV* into New Zealand some years before when there was no duty on yachts, so in that respect she should have been an attractive buy. The fact that two books and many articles had been published about her was probably a drawback, as was the fact that we intended to continue living aboard until her replacement was ready. Our brokers were understanding and never bothered us without good reason, nor did they give our whereabouts to anybody except those who appeared to be in real earnest, so we were spared the tiresome visits by people vaguely thinking about buying a yacht but who really only want to have a talk and a look around.

The first potential customer was a businessman from Wellington. He arrived on the beach near our mooring two hours before his appointment; the bunks had not been made nor the breakfast things washed up, and he stayed for five hours. We wanted cash down but he proposed a delayed method of payment which we would not accept, nevertheless he asked to be taken with his surveyor for a sail. This we did, but as well as the surveyor he brought along his teenage family; they were bored, one of them was seasick, and several times I stumbled over recumbent bodies in unexpected places. After some weeks' delay he decided not to buy but was good enough to let us see the surveyor's report. This was a strange document, more psychological than factual, but it contained the extraordinary statement that as the engine had done 4,000 hours it would need to be completely rebuilt. It was a four-cylinder Ford diesel, and by a strange coincidence I had just heard from a farming friend in England that the same type and make of engine in one of his hard-working tractors had been running without an overhaul for fifteen years and was still in good heart.

The next to come along was a rather charming married couple employed by the Bible Society to run one of its small inter-island vessels. They had lost her on one of Tonga's many reefs, and now that the insurers had paid up they were determined to find a replacement, and she must be of steel. They needed her to carry five tons of Bibles among the Pacific islands, something the old ship with her cavernous lockers could have done with ease, but they wanted her immediately.

The third customer was Stuart Clay, a tall, handsome New Zealander in his forties. Starting as a sheep shearer he had graduated to owning a large farm, worked it up and sold it. He owned the yacht *Gambol*, and had made a circumnavigation in her. While in South Africa he met Pam, a Rhodesian; she joined him and they continued the voyage together to New Zealand where they had recently got married; now they wanted a larger vessel suitable for chartering out of Tahiti or in the Caribbean, and preferably built of steel. We took the Clays for an uneventful sail and liked them; they liked the ship and, although we told them about her defects and that we were not going to move out of her yet, said they would buy her subject to survey.

That survey did not take place until we had moved to Whangarei and were living aboard in Orams' marina so as to watch over the building of our new ship and be on hand to answer questions, make decisions and consider modifications. The Clays' surveyor was knowledgeable and thorough; of course he had to investigate the trouble in the chain locker, and insisted that the cement there must first be removed. This was done with a hammer, chisel and drill by cheerful Chin, a hardworking Chinaman employed by the yard. The noise and mess was indescribable, but Susan and I stubbornly continued to live aboard. Some of the defective plating was then cut away. Unfortunately, the builders had not restricted cement to the chain locker but had carried it right through the forward bilge. The surveyor wanted that removed too, so out it had to come, revealing more corroded plating which also had to be cut away, and by evening we in the saloon could look down through the gaping holes and talk to the people working below. Meanwhile the surveyor's sharp little hammer had disclosed several places in other parts of the hull where the plating was almost rusted through; but these were small and could be welded while I kept a fire watch below, for some of the holes were close to woodwork. Of course all the damage and defects had to be made good and painted before we could go back into the water; but the yard's welders worked fast and well in spite of continuous rain and completed the work in three days. Stuart turned up the morning after the survey with the surveyor's report, and he looked so glum that we feared he was going to call off the deal. Chin was still chipping cement and a welder was using a grinder, so it was impossible to talk on board and we moved to a partly sheltered and quieter spot outside the building shed to hear what Stuart had to say. He still wanted to buy, but only if we reduced the price by a staggering $10,000. Susan and I were so unwilling to face further uncertainty and the prospect of having to take other prospective buyers out for sails and probably endure more surveys, that we scarcely hesitated before agreeing to Stuart's terms, but Susan did persuade him to pay three-quarters of the cost of the work the yard was doing.

*   *   *

Until we came to live on the yard's doorstep we had been paying weekly visits by road, and were pleased with the excellent progress being made with Job 40. This had started a little earlier than expected with young Graham, an apprentice shipwright in his fifth and final year, laying down the lines full size on the white-painted mould-loft floor. I was pleased to see that although the country had officially gone metric all measurements were in feet, inches and eighths, for lofting is a delicate operation and there is less risk of error when familiar units are used. Under Ray Roberts, Graham would be supervising the building.

When lofting was finished templates were made and the keel, stem, frames and other members were laminated, and with some temporary moulds were erected upside down and fastened together in the building shed which, because of its general shape and semi-circular roof, was known as the hay barn. The stringers were then fastened fore and aft over the frames and moulds, and the three skins of planking laid on top of them. In addition to its great strength and watertightness this method of building has other merits: because each skin is laid diagonally between keel and gunwales, only short lengths, which are easy to handle and fit, are needed and no caulking is required. There is also the interesting point that as the planking is held away from frames and bulkheads by the inch-thick stringers, there is unobstructed fore-and-aft ventilation along the planking; but this does have the drawback that if any water should manage to get below, as it might by way of a cockpit locker lid, it will—as we were to discover later—run along the stringers to the lowest point and enter lockers, instead of going straight into the bilge as it would with orthodox construction.

In the confines of the hay barn it was difficult to get much idea of what the vessel looked like except through the wide door at the end by way of which she would eventually emerge. Her stern—that very broad, flat stern—faced that way and it was only possible to see that end of her properly by facing away, bending down and peering between one's widespread legs. Doing so I thought she looked a bit odd, for the sweeping curve of the keel caught my eye and there was as yet no deadwood, false keel, or rudder post to delineate the underwater profile; nevertheless I found her disturbingly exciting. The shell of our future home in its upside down attitude was a remarkable sight when viewed from within. The diagonal planking of the inner skin, the many stringers sweeping fore and aft, the graciously curved frames, each married to its mate by a sturdy wood floor, all appeared to be hanging from the laminated keel soaring overhead. Our feet were buried in a litter of sawdust and crisp, curled planings, and the lovely, vaulted erection around and above us glowed golden in the floodlights. We might have been in some futuristic architect's dream-house or in a Samoan *fale*, except that our colours and scents were so very much better than theirs, and the perfect symmetry of the thing was breathtaking.

*   *   *

Of the many rigs from which to choose I prefer the cutter for a yacht exceeding 35 feet. The mast is more nearly amidships than it is with other rigs, and the shrouds therefore have maximum spread, though perhaps I should add that there are of course some rigs, such as the Chinese and the cat, in which the masts have no support at all, but I have no experience of them. Also the mast of the cutter is well stayed fore and aft, for as well as topmast stay and backstay there is, lower down, the inner forestay probably backed up with a pair of running backstays, and logically two pairs of crosstrees (spreaders) are provided, thus making a rigging plan of great integrity with the loads well distributed. In heavy weather the reefed mainsail and staysail, with their combined centre of effort near the centre of the vessel, provide a good rig under which to heave-to, and the mast is in the best position to allow her to remain beam on to wind and sea if she ever has to lie a-hull. There is also the point that if, with the two headsail rig, the jib is the first sail to be taken in when the wind freshens, one is still left with an efficient slot between staysail and main, whereas when the headsail of the single headsail rig is reefed or changed for a smaller one, there is a wide gap between it and the main.

However, with simplicity and general ease of handling in

mind, we chose masthead sloop rig for our new boat (Fig.1) with a total area of a little more than 700 square feet; perhaps this was a trifle small, but we did not want to be reefing for ever, and one day perhaps we would invest in a large, light-weather headsail. With this rig, when tacking or gybing there would be no runners to attend to, and only one pair of headsail sheets which would be handled by self-tailing winches.

In the past we had spent a lot of time bouncing about on wet foredecks changing headsails, but hoped not to have to do so any more as we were going to have roller furling/reefing gear for the single big headsail. These gears have come a long way since the first Wykeham Martin appeared, and with the luff of the sail held in a groove in an alloy foil, we were hoping that one of the new breed would work effectively. In New Zealand there had been some failures of such gears, at least one of them leaving the owner in the traumatic situation of being unable to furl or reef or even lower his sail in a rising wind. But many cruising people, particularly in the U.S.A., had obtained excellent service from them, and we hoped to join their ranks by getting one of the American-made Hood Seafurls.

All our earlier yachts had masts of wood, a material on which it is easy to add to or alter the position of fittings; but we felt we should now live in our day and have a mast and boom of alloy; for spars of a given section this material is lighter and stiffer than wood, and we hoped might need less maintenance.

All standing rigging was to be of 1 × 19 stainless wire, and for a time we were undecided whether to have swaged terminals or to go in for the more expensive but easily fitted Norseman type. When the last owner of the big ketch *Astral* was out sailing with us a short time before he had said that aboard the new yacht he was planning, a 110-footer, he would have only Norseman fittings because too many of *Astral*'s swages had failed. I believed, however, that swages should be satisfactory provided the terminals precisely match the wire to which they are to be attached, and that the rotary swaging machine is in good order; so that was what we would have. In my experience the threads of stainless steel rigging screws tend to gall, making adjustment difficult or even impossible, so ours would be of bronze. Halyards were to be of Marlow pre-stretched, 3-strand poly-

Fig. 1   Sail Plan. Sail areas: mainsail 325 square feet; jib 390 square feet; staysail 100 square feet; trysail 100 square feet; multi-purpose sail (not shown) 818 square feet. The alterations made to keel, sternpost and rudder are shown in dotted lines

ester, a rope which as we already knew has a long life and is remarkably chafe-resistant, and sheets of the same firm's plaited rope. Marlow Ropes Ltd generously sent out from England enough of both types for all our requirements as a gift.

I have always advocated roller reefing for the mainsail of a cruising yacht because of its simplicity, and the speed and ease with which one person can reduce sail on any point of sailing without the need to bring the boom inboard for lashings to be passed or reef points tied. It does not always produce such a well-setting sail as the other method, and complications arise if a martingale (kicking strap) is to be used when the sail is reefed, but I considered its merits far outweighed these drawbacks. However, no suitable gear could be had in New Zealand and, again with the intention of living in our time, we decided to do what everybody else did out here, and have what is today often called 'slab' or 'jiffy' reefing, i.e. the pendant and point arrangement. It appeared to be well understood, had been modernised, and the fittings were readily available. This was one of my many mistakes, and eventually we reverted to roller gear, as you shall see. I had also considered that a cruiser's mainsail should not have any roach, i.e. the leech should be straight, for then with a little bit of luck no battens are needed, and they can be a nuisance when setting or taking in a sail except when head to wind; there is also less risk of chafe from the topping lift. But here again I let myself be swayed by modern trends, and when Alan drew a mainsail with roach I let it stay – the plain fact was I rather liked the look of it; and as for those battens, well most sailmakers seem to find they need to fit them to make a sail set well.

For spars and standing rigging we chose to patronise a firm in Auckland which specialised in this work and claimed that none of the thousands of swages it had done had failed, and there were so many matters to be discussed that we had to pay them a visit. As we do not care for hotels, motels or busy city streets we went there by sea, a trip of 150 miles. Auckland Harbour is always crowded with yachts, and at that time its major marina was so disrupted by an expansion programme that a berth for the visitor was almost impossible to find. However, we knew that the Royal New Zealand Yacht

Squadron, which had recently invited us to be honorary members, kept two berths for out-of-town members; but a 'phone call from Kawau Island, where we put in on the way during a spell of bad weather, elicited the information that both visitors' berths were fully booked for at least six months, and it was suggested, quite seriously I believe, that the only way to get a berth would be to arrange in advance for a cradle and have the yacht hauled out on arrival. We then 'phoned the sparmakers who said they could accommodate us at their own wharf above the harbour bridge, so that was where we went. They were waiting for us with ropes attached to hauling-off chains, for the berth was exposed to some winds and could get rough. We had expected to see the streets and houses of suburbia crowding down to a noisy waterfront, but instead found that the wharf lay at the foot of a tree-lined bluff, and in the evening it was so quiet that we could listen to the haunting cries of waders. Although the graceful arc of orange lights denoting the harbour bridge was in full view we were out of earshot of the traffic there.

Alan had specified a mast with a section of 8 in × 5½ in, and on the plan its single pair of crosstrees struck me as being a trifle short. They allowed the shrouds to come to the masthead at an angle of 12°, but I believed that for a cruising yacht with open water in mind the angle should be not less than 15°; no doubt Alan had done this to permit the headsail to be sheeted hard in when closehauled. However, the sparmakers did some calculations based on ballast/displacement ratio, hull form and sail area, and advised that a spar of larger section (approximately 9½ in × 6 in) was called for. They did add that were the mast to be stepped on the keel, instead of on deck as it was to be, Alan's specification would have been adequate. The larger mast would weigh only 75 lb more than the smaller one. They also decided without any prompting from me that the crosstrees should be lengthened and placed a little higher up the mast, thus increasing the shroud angle at the masthead from 12° to 17°. I was happy about this because a small increase of angle rapidly reduces the load and allows more latitude when setting up the rigging. But Alan proved to have been absolutely right, for when the time came we found that we could not sheet the headsail in far enough for efficient sailing hard on the wind.

I was courteously persuaded to abandon some of my more conservative ideas. For example, I had asked for external halyards, believing they would be less subject to chafe than internal ones, easier to keep an eye on and, if necessary, to replace. But it was pointed out that the maximum number of sheaves in a standard masthead box is four, and if halyards were to be rove externally each halyard would occupy two sheaves (one forward, one aft). So two blocks would need to be slung from the masthead to take the topping lift and the spare halyard, which we thought might be a wise thing to have; such an arrangement would add to congestion at the masthead and increase the risk of chafe. By rigging the halyards internally, however, each rope would occupy only a single sheave and the whole affair would be neater, and of course would offer less wind resistance.

Although the halyard and topping lift exits from the mast could not all be at the same height, as that would have weakened the mast at that point, I asked that they be as near 7 feet above the cleats as possible, for our old bones find it safer to pull down than to pull up, and with that distance between exit and cleat one would be able to swig on the fall of a rope or even use a handy-billy, though that should rarely be necessary as there would be two open-barrel winches on the mast.

While I was considering these and other holes I did wonder if the reason why some yachts that had been knocked down onto their beam-ends were reluctant to get up again might have been that their alloy masts filled too quickly with water.

Although it was not our intention to set a spinnaker we would want to be able to boom out the headsail when running, and for that purpose asked for a 17-foot pole to be provided. Its gooseneck was to slide on a 12-foot length of track on the fore side of the mast, so that when not in use the inboard end of the spar could be hauled up the track by an endless line serving as uphaul/downhaul, and its outboard end clipped to the guardrail. The spare halyard would serve as its topping lift.

We discussed the more important matters, but I left many of the details to the people I regarded as experts, with the result that when the spars were eventually delivered to the yard and unpacked, I was horrified by some of the things that had been done or had not been done. For example, no track had been provided; instead there was the standard racing type of mast-groove so that fragile slugs would have to be used for the luff of the mainsail instead of robust slides. The oval boom was absurdly large, 8 in deep instead of $5\frac{3}{4}$ in, and it was provided with a sleeve at its fore end on which it was free to rotate 20° or so each way, presumably to allow it to take up the same lateral plane as the foot of the sail on either tack. In a cruising yacht this is undesirable and the metallic clanging the fitting made when tacking, gybing, or rolling with little wind was so disturbing that eventually we withdrew the sleeve and inserted bolts to hold it rigid. Exit boxes had not been placed where I had indicated, nor had the steaming light, which had been fitted almost at the masthead where the rolled-up headsail would obscure it over a wide arc; also the spar for booming out the headsail was far too heavy. But by the time we had discovered these and other faults there was not enough time left to return the spars to their makers for correction.

Some time later, while in Australia, we had a light-weather sail made, and as it repeatedly fouled the steaming light, although we had fitted a guard, I had to remove the light and its bracket. It seemed an impossible task to re-position the light in its proper place further down because that would have involved drilling a fair-size hole through the mast wall and into the internal alloy conduit so as to reach and pull out the correct pair of wires, and almost certainly the drill would have damaged or destroyed the insulation, calling for complete rewiring of the mast. The all-round white light incorporated in the masthead light had thereafter to serve, though not legally, as a steaming light.

I had chosen a widely-advertised brand of navigation lights because at the time it was the only one offering a strobe in the combination tricolour masthead light, and it may be recalled that during the voyage to British Columbia in *Wanderer IV* we had been much impressed with the strobe lights displayed by the salmon fishermen and decided we must have one. It seemed logical to get the rest of the navigation lights—bow-bicolour, stern, and steaming—from the same firm. One of the advertised merits of this range of lights was that, with the exception of the strobe, they all made use of halogen lamps which, it is said, give more light for a given consumption of electricity than do conventional filament lamps. The halogen lamp is very small, about $\frac{5}{8}$ in long and its two prongs are barely 1 mm in diameter. It was not until I had to replace a defective one in daylight and fine weather that I wondered how one is expected to do the job from a bosun's chair in the dark when it is raining. First two plastic screws must be taken out so that part of the light can be removed. The new lamp comes in a cardboard holder which, the instructions say, should not be removed until the lamp is plugged in, but since it fits so tightly an attempt to pull it off at once unplugs the lamp from its socket; so of course one has first to remove the cardboard and hold the lamp in one's fingers, not forgetting to wipe off any fingerprints with a clean cloth damped with alcohol. Just imagine! Then the light has to be reassembled, the two holes lined up (as there is no key to centre the light on its base one has to poke about with a spike to find them) and screws inserted and tightened. Although these lights are said to be waterproof they are not; within the first year we were to find damp had got in between the colour screen and the clear sleeve into which it was fitted, and the sleeves could not be separated for cleaning. I would have gone in for lights made by Aqua Signal, which I knew from experience were easy to open up without any tools and their bayonet-fitted lamps could be changed without even having to look, but at that time Aqua Signal did not make a masthead tricolour light incorporating a strobe–they do now.

The sparmakers supplied and fitted a pair of floodlights of unknown nationality under the crosstrees, and it was not until I had to open one of them because it had failed that I realised what a shoddy thing it was. Not even a token effort had been made to keep out rain, and it was fitted with a festoon lamp; this is cylindrical and has a cone-shaped electrode at each end to fit into holes in a pair of metal spring clips, a set-up which in my view should find no place in a seagoing vessel, though it has become almost standard in the yacht fittings sold in Australia and New Zealand, which are probably made in Taiwan. Certainly a box of a dozen spare festoon lamps which I bought were made in that country; all of them proved to be faulty, some burning out within a few seconds. The chandler showed no surprise at this, and explained that as his customers preferred them because they were a few cents cheaper than the German-made ones, he no longer stocked the latter, but he gladly got a box of them for me and none were faulty.

We had found it more difficult to select a sailmaker than a sparmaker because there were so many and we knew nothing about any of them, but finally chose Neale Dearlove (his logo was a heart which he liked to put on everything he made) because he appeared to be businesslike, his quotation was competitive, and his clean, bright loft was not far from the builder's yard. After our return passage north from Auckland, which was not enjoyable because of lack of wind, a very heavy swell and unusually poor visibility, we called on Neale and were astonished to find him making sails of fluorescent orange material that felt almost as hard and stiff as plywood, but were relieved when he explained that this was not his choice but that of a customer who was building a 40-footer and had been reading about the heavy weather Fastnet race of 1979. I am of the opinion that many cruising yachts and their people are badly handicapped by sails which are too stiff and heavy. With good quality polyester the strength of a sail should lie more in the design, stitching and general workmanship that goes into it than in the weight of the cloth. We gathered round Neale's desk, and while his spaniel licked our bare feet ('No shoes in the loft, please') discussed cut and material, and chose a soft Bainbridge cloth dyed a rich tan. We decided on $7\frac{1}{4}$ ounce cloth for the mainsail and $6\frac{3}{4}$ ounce for the headsail, the manufacturers having advised that they would not recommend a lighter cloth for a headsail of the size of ours if it is to be reefed. These weights are American, and their British equivalents are $9\frac{1}{4}$ ounce and $8\frac{1}{2}$ ounce respectively.

Although the yacht was to be basically a sloop, I had sketched in on the sailplan a staysail of 100 square feet. This was intended for use in heavy weather or in the event of trouble with the roller furling/reefing gear of which I was mistrustful, though it might also be of value in providing additional sail area on a reach, thus turning the yacht temporarily into a cutter. Its stay, secured to a tang on the mast just above the crosstrees, would normally be made fast by its fibre rope tail out of the way at a pinrail inside the chainplates, and when the sail was to be used the stay would be set up by a three-part tackle. Neale recommended that the same weight of cloth as for the mainsail should be used for the little sail.

* * *

On our return to the yard we found that Ray had been keeping things moving during our fortnight's absence (the third skin was going on), and his wife Barbara, who efficiently kept the firm's accounts, had another little bill ready for us. Susan and I then settled down to design and draw to scale the accommodation plan of our choice, and soon discovered this to be one of the most intriguing but frustrating things that we had ever attempted.

It is comparatively easy to do as some agents do when advertising production yachts, by taking an outline drawing of the yacht and sketching in roomy lockers, wide bunks, a spacious galley and fine bookshelves right up against the firm lines of the plan, and it is astonishing how much can be fitted in like that. But of course we knew that the outline showed only the outboard edges of the deck, and that to allow for wood construction we must move the lines inboard about $2\frac{1}{4}$ inches each side to accommodate the thickness of the planking and stringers. Then lower down the lines depicting the plane of the load waterline came remorselessly inboard towards each end, for of course the yacht had overhangs and the topsides some flare. The cabin sole, which was 17 inches below the LWL, though certainly wide amidships, tapered away to nothing long before it reached the bow and stern. It soon became clear even to our untrained eyes that we must revise some of our ideas on accommodation because our new floating home was going to have nothing like so much internal volume as our old one.

Our basic requirements were: a self-draining cockpit with bridge-deck, a workable seagoing galley, a chart table with flat stowage under it for many charts, a gracious saloon with plenty of lockers and bookshelves, a large table and a heating stove; a separate sleeping place, and a heads. As the engine was the only item the size and shape of which was known and could not be altered, we started with that, placing it as far aft as possible and designing its casing in such a way that access for servicing would be easy; this casing had a bearing on the position of the companionway and galley.

We believed that with a weatherly and easily driven hull, we did not need a very powerful engine, and working on the old British assumption (which I fancy is now quite out of date) that for an able sailing yacht one horse-power per ton of displacement should be enough, and that two horse-power per ton would be generous, we decided on a 20 horse-power engine for our 11 tons.

We might have chosen a European or American engine, but New Zealand had been steadily growing closer to Japan in trade relations, and because of their ready availability and the ease with which spare parts could be obtained, Japanese engines were popular. As Orams Marine were agents for the Yanmar range of diesels and had several in stock, we took one of them, a two-cylinder model of the horse-power we required. This had the merit that it was provided with decompressors and a handle, so that in the event of starter-motor or electrical failure it could be got going by hand—so long as a muscular young man was available. It looked neat and compact, was freshwater cooled, weighed 420 lb and would drive a 17 in × 13 in two-blade propeller through 2:1 reduction gear.

We did not look forward to sharing our living quarters with a diesel engine, particularly after enjoying the luxury of a separate heat-, sound- and smell-proof engine-room with full kneeling headroom, but there was no alternative, and later we fitted a wood baffle and a lot of sound-deadening material to reduce the noise. The bridge-deck had to be wide enough fore-and-aft to accommodate beneath it two large-capacity, heavy-duty batteries, which would be charged by the engine's 35-amp alternator. With the intention of reducing in-port charging to the minimum time, I arranged with the electrician to fit a bypass so that the charging regulator could be cut out, thus enabling the batteries to be charged at a higher continuous rate while I kept a check on them with thermometer and hydrometer; but although I provided a wiring diagram the bypass was not a success, probably because the diodes were incorporated in the alternator instead of being in a separate regulator.

The cockpit was to be small—in the end it turned out wider than intended because I foolishly agreed to the coach roof being wider than it should have been—and its seats were to hinge up for access to the lockers under them. The locker to starboard was for the two gas (LPG) bottles whose cocks would be reached by leaning out through the companionway and lifting the lid; it would be gas-tight and drain into the cockpit. The port locker, through which, provided I did not put on weight, I hoped to be able to crawl round into the otherwise inaccessible space abaft the cockpit, was intended for the storage of ropes, fenders and other gear.

I drew in double coamings with cave lockers for winch handles and sail tiers, and placed them far enough apart so that sheet winches and cleats could be mounted on top. At their forward ends there were to be baffles to form water-trap ventilators for the engine and the space under the bridge deck, where as well as the batteries there would be one fuel tank (the other would be outboard of the LPG locker), the loop of the exhaust system, and engine requisites such as oil, grease and distilled water. The companionway steps would hinge up to give access to this space.

I was not at all sure that it was an advantage to be living aboard one yacht while trying to design the insides of another of half the displacement. Certainly some of the vital dimensions, such as the height of seats and working surfaces, the width of bunks and doors, the depth of bookshelves, the slope of back rests, could readily be checked, but there was a strong urge to try to incorporate in the new all the best features of the old, and of course they would not fit.

Some difficult decisions confronted us, such as the matters of cooking and refrigeration. Should the cooker be mounted on pivots allowing it to swing on its fore-and-aft axis, and so remain upright at all angles of heel, or should it be fixed? The theoretical advantages of a swinging cooker with its always level hotplate and oven are obvious; but it requires a lot of space in which to swing, for in rough weather centrifugal force will fling it to an angle possibly exceeding 50° even though the angle of heel or roll may be no more than 15 or 20°, and if it were then to touch something the utensils would be thrown off; in addition its balance is upset when the oven door is opened. There might also be some risk of a gas leak because a flexible pipe must be used with it. Some experienced seagoing cooks—Lin Pardey of *Seraffyn* is one—favour a fixed cooker because it eliminates the above disadvantages, but it must be fitted with individual pot-holders as well as fiddles, and it needs to be situated fore or aft of the cook to avoid the risk of burns from spilt scalding food. The oven door should be in the athwartships plane, otherwise when on one tack the oven's contents will fall out immediately the door is opened; also, of course, it is difficult to keep the cooking utensils horizontal, thus making frying difficult, while a loaf baking in the oven may rise lopsided. We had swinging cookers in our earlier yachts, and this time would have tried a fixed one, but juggle as we might we could find no way of arranging the galley to accommodate it.

We had grown accustomed to firm butter, cold milk and fresh meat when in port because we had been using a paraffin (kerosene) burning, absorption-type refrigerator with success for eleven years. Certainly we had been concerned about the fire risk, the more so when we learnt that many homes in Australia's outback, where such refrigerators were widely used, had been destroyed by fire due, it was said, to the units exploding. Even so we might have installed one again had there been room enough, but it required a space two feet square and three feet high well ventilated on all sides, and we could not manage that.

The alternative was to have one of the mechanical type with its compressor belt-driven by the engine, but there was scarcely room for a compressor in the bilge immediately forward of the engine, where it would have to go, and even if there had been we would not have wanted to run the engine every day, perhaps twice a day, to keep the temperature down. Besides, these installations were still far from perfect, and we had observed that the majority of the ocean-going yachts that got stuck in port longer than intended nearly always had a refrigeration engineer in attendance. Perhaps an ice box would be more sensible, so I drew one in on the galley plan, and although I made it as large as possible it looked so small that I reckoned when we put ice in it there would be little room for much else. Later we were to find that ice is by no means always available, and is often uneconomic. The flaked variety used in fishing vessels does not last long, nor does 'party' ice, which is expensive. Probably the best source is a cooperative butcher who is prepared to place containers of convenient size and shape – ice-cream cartons or small plastic buckets perhaps – in his deep-freeze chamber. However, as Susan had for many years kept house ashore and afloat without the help of ice or refrigeration she supposed she would be able to do so again, but would buy ice when she could.

Originally we had thought of having a fresh water shower like we had in *Wanderer IV*, requiring pressurised water heated either by the engine or a geyser and a pump to empty the shower tray. But this seemed a ridiculously complicated and expensive way of washing ourselves, especially when we remembered that during the years we lived in an Elizabethan cottage in Berkshire we had managed to keep reasonably clean using a bucket, a kettle of hot water and a sponge. We could do better than that, though, and instead of the sponge we would use an orchardist's spray while standing in a basin in the heads where we would have the floor fibreglassed to make it water-tight, and the sponge could serve to mop up the spillage. For those who may not know of it, an orchardist's spray consists of a container holding about a gallon of water which is pressurised by a built-in hand-pump; the water comes out by way of a flexible pipe, at the end of which is a finger-controlled valve and an adjustable rose. One can get a good shower with less than half a gallon. In the tropics we would use the spray in the cockpit after swimming, but in cooler places take our showers more modestly in the heads after filling the container with warm water.

For many years our Baby Blake WCs had worked with unfailing reliability. Now, with simplicity and lack of main-tenance in mind, we would have a Lavac. This neat affair has no valves to open or close before or after use, no glands to pack, and a simple diaphragm pump evacuates the bowl and, by creating a vacuum (the seat and cover are fitted with neoprene

seals), draws in clean water. One must not pump while sitting
on it or it will be impossible to get up until the vacuum breaks,
as a buxom friend once discovered and in a panic called for
help. Since the Lavac comes from Blake and Son of Gosport,
the firm that makes the famous 'Baby', we expected it to be
reliable, and so it proved to be.

For the 17 years that we owned and voyaged in the 30-foot
sloop *Wanderer III* we used the saloon settees to sit on by day and
sleep on by night, promising ourselves that one day in a larger
vessel we would have a separate sleeping cabin with bunks
ready made up for weary bodies to tumble into. We had that
amenity in *Wanderer IV* and of course needed it in her successor,
but I did realise as I drew it on the plan what a wonderfully
spacious workshop/darkroom we might have had instead. For
a workbench I would have to use the large but not very
accessible space forward of the sleeping berths on top of the
chain locker and beyond, and as a photographic darkroom I
would have to make do with the heads, and although that
compartment was only $4\frac{1}{2}$ feet $\times$ $3\frac{1}{2}$ feet, and some of it taken up
by lockers, I did manage to use it with success, rigging up
temporary benches for enlarger and dishes, and there made
many prints for reproduction in magazines.

We had laid all this and the rest of the accommodation down
on paper in both plan and section (Ray said he had not seen
such detailed drawings before) and had got most things nicely
settled, when Alan told us that while checking the sail plan he
had found it desirable to move the mast six inches further
forward. A minor alteration, you will agree, but in its new
position the mast support would effectively block access to the
heads, and the only practical solution seemed to be to add six
inches to the galley (at least that would allow the ice box to be a
little bigger) and then shift everything else that much further
forward and take six inches off the forepeak.

All the measuring, drawing, fitting in and then re-drawing
took a lot of time, but when we proudly showed the revision to
Ray he gave it one quick look and said: 'That won't do. We've
already laminated the frames, and the bulkhead at station five
by the mast must remain as it is.'

So back we went to the drawing board with station five

haunting us, and tried again, incorporating some suggestions made by Ray to gain the odd inches here and there and lose them somewhere else. The sketch plan (Fig. 2), from which many of the details have been omitted for clarity, shows the final arrangement.

Our fresh water requirements were that we should carry as much as possible in three tanks, but how much this would be nobody could say until we filled them for the first time using a two-gallon container, and discovered that the total capacity was 105 gallons. The tanks, which had to be shallow and wide, were to be of stainless steel, two in the bilge amidships and one under the cockpit. They would be interconnected so that all could be filled through a single filler via the cockpit tank, which was the higher, and after filling, each tank would be isolated from the others by 'Clincher' ball valves. These are made in a variety of metals by the Jamesbury Corporation, in Worcester, U.S.A. They are smooth in operation, need no maintenance and require only a quarter turn of the lever to open or close. The firm's managing director, whom we had met many years ago while cruising in his waters, on learning from a magazine that we were having a new boat, kindly offered to give us all the valves we needed. We used them on the fuel pipes as well as for the fresh water, but unfortunately could not have them as sea-cocks on the nine skin fittings because of a slight difference of thread, and so there we had to fit conventional cone valves. All water would be drawn from the lowest tank by 'Whale Flipper' pumps, one in the galley and another at the basin in the heads. When a pump sucked air we would know that one tank was empty and could then open a cock on one or other of the two remaining tanks to let its contents run into the lower tank. All the piping was to be of plastic, which is light and easy to fit or replace, and on my plumbing drawing I showed that the air vents, which were to discharge into the space between the cockpit double coamings, were to be of large size, otherwise pressure could build up in a tank during filling from a high pressure supply.

Incidentally, it astonished me that such a simple little vessel needed, as I mentioned above, as many as nine holes in her hull each guarded by a sea-cock, but I could find no satisfactory way

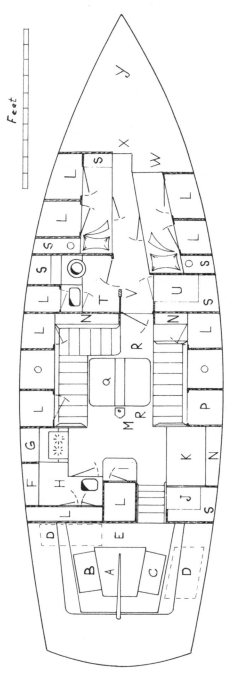

Fig. 2 Accommodation Plan. A, Self-draining cockpit, water tank under; B, hinged seat, access to port and stern lockers; C, hinged seat, access to LPG locker, two 20-lb bottles; D, fuel tanks under; E, bridge deck, batteries, exhaust loop and engine requisites under; F, pantry; G, saucepans; H, galley bench, ice box and locker under; I, portable engine casing; J, oilskin locker and bilge pump; K, chart table, chart stowage under; L, lockers; M, diesel cabin heater; N, bookshelves; O, open to yacht's side; P, chest of three drawers; Q, table with portable fiddles and fold-down leaves; R, water tanks under cabin sole; S, shelves; T, heads; U, wardrobe; V, mast support; W, work bench; X, chain locker under bench; Y, sails.

of reducing their number. They served the following purposes:
inlet and outlet for the WC, outlet for the wash-basin in the
heads, outlet for the galley sink, inlet for engine cooling water,
engine exhaust outlet, inlet for the deck-wash pump (I had
thought of combining this with the engine intake but the
engineer was against it) and two cockpit drains. However, I did
eliminate what would have been a tenth hole by having the
bilge pump discharge into the self-draining cockpit.

Our next job was to draw the deck plan, and light and
ventilation figured largely on this. In addition to the sliding
companionway hatch with perspex top and washboard, we
would have two hatches of the Maurice Griffiths double-
coaming type; they too would have perspex tops but their side
flaps were to be of lexan, a similar transparent material which is
much stronger. One would be located over the galley and the
other, acting also as a forehatch, over the sleeping cabin. Dick
McIlvride made them for us of totara, a handsome New
Zealand timber which is not subject to warping and is much
used for cabinet work. Originally we had considered fitting the
modern, low-profile alloy-frame hatches, but the only ones
available had tinted tops which we do not like as they make it
gloomy down below. However, it was their lack of hinged side
flaps and the impossibility of fitting these essential appendages
that entirely ruled them out, for such hatches have to be closed
for every shower of rain if there is wind, and for every dash of
spray. I know that some people overcome this defect by fitting
canvas covers with side flaps, but this seems a tiresome
makeshift arrangement when properly designed hatches capable of providing both light and air under most conditions can
be built. To let more light into the saloon a rectangle of the
cabin top was to be cut away and replaced with a non-opening
pane of lexan, and there were to be two prismatic deck lights
over the forepeak.

It would have been good to make all of the 12 ports in the
cabin top coamings to open, but the cost was so high that we
economised by making do with only seven of them opening.
The only metal-framed ones available were of a poor shape,
narrow with oval ends instead of being generous rectangles. We
thought we should buy the better shaped plastic type, which

looked clean and neat and were provided with fly-screens as standard. However before coming to a decision we were fortunate enough to be invited aboard an American yacht fitted with them, and although only one year old these plastic ports were already showing cracks and pieces were breaking away. So we bought the metal-framed ones and within a year their chrome plating started to peel off. Any leaks from them, or condensation, would be collected by grab-rail drip-catchers running the full length of the cabin top coamings.

I drew in a watertrap vent over the heads and, aware that in a wooden yacht rot is most likely to occur in the poorly ventilated ends, put a mushroom vent right aft and a big cowl, which could be replaced by a screw-in deck plate before going to sea, right forward.

In New Zealand 'turnover' day is an occasion almost as important as the launching. The upside down hull, now sheathed in epoxy and dynel, was jacked up under the supervision of Ray. He was a dynamo of organisation and active ability, but with a laudable concern for the safety of his men. He placed the hull on a six-wheel chassis (for which he had traded a case of rum) and drew it out by tractor into the sunshine of a perfect autumn day to where a mobile crane stood waiting. An arrangement of slings was passed around, the crane's diesel rumbled into life, and the shell was lifted clear of the chassis. There was a short pause as it swung there upside down for the last time in its life (we hoped). The crane driver, who turned out to be Ray's brother-in-law, transferred the load on the slings from one side to the other and suddenly, with a protesting creak, the shell rolled over, hung for a moment on its beam-ends, then bobbed right way up.

I thought it looked lovely, but then one of the doubts that had plagued me at three o'clock in the morning assailed me. Was it perhaps a trifle fine forward and a shade too full aft? No, it was more than just a shade; the hull looked positively fat in the quarters. I recalled that Weston Martyr, with similar doubts, secretly moved all of his *Southseaman*'s inside ballast as far aft as he could stow it before her launch. I could not do that because there would be no inside ballast, but then I also remembered that as a result of Martyr's interference his ship nearly sank by the stern at her launching, and I felt a little easier.

Gently lowered onto the chassis, the shell was shored up and wheeled back into the dim hay barn where a small, lost, black-and-white cat crouched watching with wide amber eyes. I was glad to see that Job 40 was still in the traditional attitude with her stern towards the water. Ray and Graham made a quick inspection and reported that no damage had been done during the acrobatics.

Before attending the beer drinking celebration for all hands in the yard mess that evening, Susan and I climbed a ladder and looked down into the now apparently much shrunken inside of our ship, and wondered if our carefully planned accommodation would ever fit into it.

*   *   *

Depression and delight alternated as building proceeded—depression during the weeks when nothing much seemed to happen, delight when all manner of things came together in a rush. The making of the lead keel evoked a combination of the two.

Working from the line drawing and table of offsets, Graham fabricated a smooth plug of feather-light polystyrene and a concrete specialist was called in to make a plaster of Paris mould on the plug. This was placed in a grave Graham had dug just outside the hay barn, and cement was poured in round it; but something went wrong and defects had to be patched up next day. Then the rain came. Not entirely successful attempts, including the use of an electric fire, were made to keep the mould dry, and daily we went to see how it was getting on as a doctor might a bed-ridden patient.

After a delay of a couple of weeks the weather improved and it was decided to pour. A cauldron erected near one end of the mould was filled well above the brim with a pile of 52 lb pigs of lead, and a huge fire, which eventually consumed most of the offcuts in the yard, was built beneath. A young apprentice cut the wood with a chain-saw; Chin the powerful Chinaman split the larger pieces with an axe, Graham fed it into the roaring furnace, Ru the engineer stood by to open the valve when the pigs suddenly started to melt and collapse (which they did early in the afternoon) and Ray directed operations.

It was an exciting moment when the valve was opened and in a lovely stream the molten lead began to flow from cauldron to mould – liquid silver it might have been, for it had cost almost as much. Pig after pig was fed into the cauldron (what satisfaction the Crusaders must have had) but bubbles were the problem; as the lead flowed into the still-damp mould they rose and exploded, and Ray repeatedly had to caution his people to keep out of range. Half an hour or so later the mould was brimming.

It was thought best to take the keel to the hull rather than bring the hull outdoors; so, after the keel had cooled it was to have been lifted out of the ground by a crane with a long proboscis and placed on skids beside the hull in the hay barn. But shortly before this should have taken place the crane broke down, and the smaller one that came instead was able only to lift the casting out of the ground, weigh it – it was almost exactly the designed 8,830 lb – and set it down on blocks. Graham worked on it for more than a week, fairing it up, filling depressions and drilling holes for the bolts; I watched and did not envy him. Meanwhile, of the three water tanks, the two that were to go in the bilge could not be fitted until the keel bolts were in, and joinery work was awkward. However, in time the broken crane was mended and the keel was bolted on, tanks fitted and connected, and the sole replaced.

How fortunate Susan and I were to be living aboard our old ship in the marina belonging to the yard where our new one was being built, for not only could we watch her growing and get most of the details done the way we wanted them, but we were able to play a small part, cleaning out the sawdust and shavings at each day's end with brush and vacuum cleaner; the yard employees had no objection to us doing this, indeed the people working on Job 40 expressed their pleasure at finding everything clean and tidy when they turned up in the morning, and were grateful when we discovered tools they had mislaid or were buried in rubbish. As well as asking us to do this, Ray had invited us to do all the internal and on-deck painting and varnishing, thus saving us considerable expense; again nobody minded. It did feel strange to start our daily labours just as everybody else was knocking off, and apart from the hum of the vacuum cleaner the hay barn was unnaturally silent; but usually we had the company of the little black-and-white cat who received many a tasty handout there and had taken up permanent residence. In working hours she could often be seen closely supervising a job, and she appeared to enjoy the ear-splitting din of mechanical tools, but the chattering sparrows that roosted on the rafters infuriated her as they were out of reach.

Our close association enabled us, indeed almost forced us to gain an intimate knowledge of every nook and corner of our new boat; we discovered with our sore finger tips where glue had oozed to form sharp stalactites along the stringers or in the limber holes, and removed them with a chisel; we could spot any areas where the wood preservative was thin or missing, and make them good, and in less active moments try to decide in which lockers our various belongings should be stowed.

About once a week we cleaned up the earth floor, using a rake, two bits of wood and a barrow, and tidied the work benches, and then realised that some of the cost of building a boat has to cover waste. The abrasive paper used for sanding (rubbing down) came in big rolls of several grades which were slung up on spindles convenient for people to pull out and cut off their needs; we often found lengths of this which had scarcely been used before being discarded, and collected enough for our own requirements for many a day. After Chin had painted the top strake green Ray was not entirely happy with it – he wanted the finish to be perfect everywhere – and at the weekend he came along to do it himself. For the many hours he worked at this and other things he did for the ship he never made a charge. On this occasion he brought with him a very special brush and some sheets of fine grit paper; each sheet he folded into four, used one quarter for a couple of quick rubs, tossed it down to the floor and took another. When he had finished painting he put the brush on the bench and said to Susan, 'You'd better make a proper job of cleaning this, it's cost you fifteen dollars.'

The thinner/cleaning fluid for the two-pot polyurethane paint being used was almost as expensive as the paint itself, and

Susan needed a lot of it to clean that brush thoroughly. However the next day she discovered that someone had used the brush with a two-pot mix and left it uncleaned, rigid and useless on the bench – Barbara must have heard about this, for the cost of that brush did not appear on the monthly bill. After Ray had left we collected enough of his discarded paper to keep us supplied for a long time. One of the younger apprentices, known to us as 'Botcher' John because he made a mess of most things he tried to do, was in the habit of leaving the lids off cans of paint, glue, preservative and filler so that their contents were spoiled. I have seen similar waste in other yards; no doubt it is inevitable, and it accounts for only a tiny proportion of the total cost, but I did sometimes wonder if the offenders would be quite so casual if they had to buy the materials.

As well as those dusty evenings, the daylight hours were fully occupied by the new boat, for gear and fittings had to be selected and obtained, and the many problems sorted out as and when they arose. For instance, there was no deck construction plan to show where the beams should be, it being left to Graham to space them as he thought best, having regard to the various strains imposed. This was fine, but it resulted in the galley skylight being fitted farther aft than I had intended, and now there was not enough room abaft it in which to fit an athwartships track with a sliding car for the lower mainsheet block. The sheet would therefore have to lead from the extreme end of the boom, which involved telling the sparmakers to increase the length of that spar by a foot (fortunately it had not yet been made), and the fitting of an old-fashioned horse aft to carry the block over the tiller.

We had intended to have a ceiling of white, matt Formica fastened across the under sides of the cabin top beams to provide an insulating air space between it and the deck, but when we saw the pale clean beauty of the beams which Graham had cut from a balk of kauri it seemed a pity to cover them with anything but varnish. So it was agreed that the Formica should be glued to the deck before that was laid on the beams. As the deck was of two layers of $\frac{1}{2}$-inch ply glued to one another, we trusted that condensation would be minimal even without insulation, but some time later a winter spent in New Zealand

showed that we should not have let aesthetics outweigh practi-
cality, for of a chilly morning the whole deckhead, including the
inside of lockers, dripped water unless the cabin heater was
alight, and the mattresses in the sleeping cabin grew damp.
The deck was left off while the electrician wove his web of wires,
many of which he laid in a gutter cut in the top of the king
plank, and some were of such small gauge that I fussed about a
voltage drop in the longer runs. We were thankful for the delay
in putting on the deck because painting by artificial light
(brush in one hand and wander-lead lamp in the other) is not
easy or satisfactory, and we had to work fast to keep pace with
the speedy joiners and could do so only at weekends when we
had the boat to ourselves and there was no dust.

We had planned to carry the 7½-foot dinghy capsized amidships on the cabin top abaft the mast, but had quite overlooked
the chimney of the heating stove which would then have
emerged inside it. So the dinghy stowage had to be shifted to
port and the chimney to starboard; we would have preferred to
move those items the other way, for then the dinghy could be
launched on the same (starboard) side as the boarding ladder is
traditionally rigged, but then it would have covered the lexan
light-admitting pane.

We had decided to install a diesel-burning cabin heater and
particularly wanted one made by Dickinson. This Canadian
firm had specialised in that type of heater for many years, and
when we were in Canada it was rare to find a yacht without one
of that make. I had written to Dickinson about this, but as they
could not reply by mail because the Canadian postal workers
were on strike they telexed the firm of Unwin, which operated a
fleet of fishing vessels out of Bluff in the South Island; their fleet
was fitted with Dickinson heaters, and Unwin had a spare one
which, within a few days, was ours. It was made entirely of
stainless steel, and as it was 30 inches high (the same height as
the saloon table) and only 8 inches wide, I designed the table in
such a way that its after leg would accommodate the heater.
Had the table been made of solid mahogany, like much of the
rest of the joinery work, the heat would probably have caused it
to warp; but custom board, which does not warp, was used
instead, and we chose a piece with an attractive whorled-grain

mahogany veneer which looked particularly pleasing by lamp-light. The heater, as one might have expected, proved a good investment, though with a maximum output of 8,000 BTUs, which is said to be sufficient to heat 1,000 cubic feet, it is perhaps a little small for us. Its only drawback is that it takes about 20 minutes to light, but in Canada this would be no disadvantage, for there it is customary to light up at the beginning of winter and keep the stove going until spring arrives. In New Zealand one normally needs a heater only in the winter mornings and evenings.

Bob and Roy, the cheerful team working on the below-deck joinery, were boat owners, so of course they had their own ideas as to how things should be done. Most of these were sound and practical, like Bob's thoughtful suggestion that he make a small recess in the galley skirting below the sink so that Susan would not stub her toes while washing up, and Roy's idea of finishing off the half bulkheads with mahogany pillars which he turned on a lathe to his own simple and graceful design. Nevertheless we had to keep a weather eye lifting, for occasionally someone could be so concerned that the final appearance should please him as a craftsman that he might overlook the practical use of the item at sea. Fiddles were an example of this, and the sample they showed us was vertical on the outside and sloping inside, which would have been just right for encouraging a cup or plate to slide up and over.

Sometimes when we found an important job of engineering or building had been done not quite as we would have liked it there was a temptation to ask for it to be done again; but unless it was essential this had to be resisted because of cost, for as I have already mentioned we were paying the hourly rate for all labour. In most circumstances we considered it best not to interfere, particularly with things we did not fully understand, but to let the yard go ahead and do them in the manner to which it was accustomed, though sometimes the result caused us concern.

I mistrusted the exhaust system through which the injected water was forced to run uphill, fearing that it might run back and draw in seawater to flood the engine when it was stopped. I therefore made a mental note to close the cock on the exhaust pipe immediately the engine was stopped, but of course the risk then is that one might forget to open it before restarting. We overcame this by taking out the starting key and hanging it up elsewhere immediately the cock was closed, as a reminder.

Susan was worried by the design and fastening of the chainplates for the backstay bridle, I about the watertightness of the chainplates for the shrouds, as they had been put in through the deck and relied on silicone rubber alone to stop them leaking instead of on caulking. We were both astonished one evening to find that a pair of hanging knees in way of the mast had not been placed under the same deck beam.

Our friend Noel Barrott was the senior shipwright in the yard; he was skilful and efficient and the only employee on a staff of 20 with extensive seagoing experience. Recently, he and his wife, in their engineless yacht *Massin'a*, which Noel had built in his spare time while working as an apprentice, completed one of the bravest and most competent circumnavigations of the decade. This great voyage included Alaska, Cape Horn and the Falklands, a year in England, where Noel worked for Souters in Cowes, the Cape, a dramatic visit to ice-bound, uninhabited Heard Island in 53°S, and a return to New Zealand by way of the Forties and Tasmania. So far as I am aware this splendid, unsponsored achievement received no recognition, but perhaps that was as Noel would wish, for he is a modest man. He was not working on our boat but was in charge of the building of a big Herreshoff ketch in the neighbouring shed, and now and then was kind enough to come over and give us his advice. When we drew his attention to those hanging knees he laughed and said, 'Regard them as purely cosmetic; the bulkheads are strong enough not to need them.'

For me a typical day at the yard was something like this: the marina walkway is slippery with frost as I make my way ashore at 0730 to find Bob, who, supervised by the black-and-white cat, is about to fit the complicated pantry he has been making to my design. I suggest that first he might run the gas pipe to the cooker behind it; he nods and asks if I want plastic or copper; I say copper, all in one length. Pipe-smoking Roy has temporarily fitted the companionway ladder he constructed, a fine affair of solid mahogany which I plan to take away and varnish in a dust-free place. I ask for a modification which will alow me a bit more room when servicing the engine, and he readily agrees.

A few days before Graham had completed his apprenticeship and, to celebrate his elevation to shipwright status, his mates had tossed him fully clad into the river. In the evening he gave a 'shout' (a drinks party) for all hands and remembered to bring along plenty of fish and chips. I find him preparing to plane the teak rail capping and he wants to know what section I have in mind. I say, 'It already looks a bit mean, so don't remove more than you must.' The rudder is being hung for the third (or is it the fourth?) time after further modifications. Probably it is because they are not acquainted with the outboard rudder, which I had thought would be so simple to make, that the building and hanging of it has been frustrating and time-consuming, and no bottom pintle has been provided to ship into the keel in the traditional manner. I ask Graham to let into the blade a 5 lb lump of lead we had carried around for years, to offset some of the rudder's tendency to float. Later it is suggested that we might like to have a spare tiller made while the jig was still set up. I reply rather crossly that there is nothing the matter with the tiller–a massive laminate of teak and kauri–the weakness lies in the rudder head, so they had better bore a $\frac{3}{4}$-in hole in the blade to enable us to reeve a steering rope if the rudder head collapses.

Back on board *Wanderer IV* I find Susan entertaining a nice young man from Cleveco Murray, who has arrived with an unexpected present of four of his firm's fine winches. We persuade him to share our cheese lunch, during which he discovers that we do not care much for chrome plate, so he says he will take the winches away and replace them with ones with a polished bronze finish (which he did).

When Susan and I visit the hay barn in the afternoon we see things have been moving. Bob has run the gas pipe, though not along the route we had selected because a fuel tank was in the way, has fitted the pantry, and is fixing sliding doors to a galley locker. Do we want a hole in each for a finger grip? I tell him we have a pair of neat alloy grips and go back home to get them.

Roy, having finished with the companionway ladder, has been fitting the echo-sounder transducer. Its cable is too short to permit it to be fitted where its makers recommend, just forward of the keel, so as the cable must not be lengthened except at the factory, which is in the U.S.A., the transducer has to go beside the keel and therefore farther outboard, where the angle of the planking is steeper. Roy was not aware that the transducer must not be more than 20° out of the vertical. Unfortunately it is, so out it has to come so that packing wedges may be inserted. Then we find the threaded part of the transducer housing is too short, apparently because the makers imagine that all boats are built of grp.

Ray, making his afternoon rounds, wants us to mark on the cabin top coamings the positions for the seven opening and five non-opening ports. I point out that as the coamings have a little tumblehome the opening ports must be fitted with wedge-shaped packing pieces to hold them vertical, otherwise water will lodge in the deep metal frames and run inboard when a port is opened. He agrees. I ask if he has any news of the masthead tricolour/strobe light and the galley and washbasin pumps, all ordered from a chandler six months ago. He shakes his head as an electric saw drowns his voice. When the din stops I say to hell with the chandler, I will order direct from California and Belfast (what a pleasure it was a few days later to deal with friendly, efficient firms and receive the equipment by air within two weeks).

The knocking-off whistle has blown, but nobody seems in much of a hurry to leave, most preferring to finish whatever they are doing, and Roy wants a word with us about the handrail/drip-catcher he will be starting on in the morning. Then Dan arrives up on the staging to talk about the pulpit. He is the yard's stainless steel artist, and is determined to get everything, including stanchions and pushpit, right first time, and he points out that a pulpit is a tricky thing to design because it must be considered in three dimensions. He makes a pencil sketch on a boatyard scribbling pad (a plywood offcut) to show why the forward lower rail of the pulpit should be omitted, otherwise it could foul the shank of the anchor when the latter is being brought inboard. He says he will give it some thought overnight. By now daylight is rapidly fading, and with the floodlights switched on Susan and I start to clean up the day's mess.

*   *   *

Each time a New Zealand-registered yacht wishes to obtain clearance to sail for another country, she must first pass an inspection and be provided with certain equipment. Susan and I did not hold with this, believing that it was up to us to decide whether or not our vessel was fit to go to sea, and our trust in yacht inspectors had been shaken by the man who fitted the rudder and weakened it by cutting pieces out to accommodate the pintles, and who fitted one of the sea-cocks in such a manner that it could not be fully closed – for he was a yacht inspector. Also, we believed that the mandatory life-raft, ship/shore radio, rockets and flares, dan-buoy and lifebuoys placed the emphasis not so much on safety as on rescue, a tenet with which we heartily disagree. Rather than have to rescue a person we consider it is very much better to prevent him going overboard in the first place by, for example, having guardrails at least 30 inches high instead of the low ones permitted in New Zealand. We prefer to put our money into good sails and rigging and efficient ground tackle, and should we find ourselves in difficulties we would hope to extract ourselves by our own unaided efforts rather than call for help.

The obvious way of avoiding the regulations would be to have our new yacht registered not in New Zealand but in England, then as a British ship she would not be subject to the New Zealand rules. To get this done we had to choose a port of registry, and since I was born in Southampton and our earlier yachts had been registered there, that was the port we selected. We asked for the name *Wanderer V* to be approved, giving our reasons: For the past 40 years all our yachts had the name *Wanderer (I, II, III* and *IV)*; they had all figured in books and talks, and one in films and on television, so naturally we wished to retain the name for the sake of continuity, goodwill and sentiment. However, the Registrar decreed that the name would not be approved unless we sold *Wanderer IV* to a foreigner (Stuart and Pam Clay, who were buying her, were New

Zealanders and therefore not foreigners) when she would automatically be removed from the register, or unless we changed her name. This we would not do because we believe any ship should be entitled to keep her name (as had all our other *Wanderers*), the more so when she had made it widely known, and Stuart and Pam did not want the name to be changed either. Southampton's argument was that there must not be more than one of any name in the register. So we approached a higher authority in Cardiff. He said yes, we could have the name provided the registry of *Wanderer IV* was changed from British to New Zealand. The Clays had no objection to this, so it was done.

Many steps had then to be taken and many forms completed, but as I understand it this time-consuming process is now to be simplified. The cost was considerable. For example, we had to apply to Southampton for a surveyor to take the necessary measurements; they appointed Mac MacGuire, then sailing master of the *Bounty* replica, which had been built in Whangarei for another Captain Bligh film. She lay quarter of a mile from the yard, and I suppose Mac took no more than half an hour to come along, take the three required measurements—length, beam and depth—and return to his ship, yet the charge for this service, payable to Lloyd's in Southampton, was £175. I don't suppose Mac got much of it. For us the total cost of the paperwork was £350.

We wanted the name to be carved and it would have to be done three times, once for each bow and once for the stern. When *Wanderer IV* was being built in Holland we provided a full-size drawing of her name in the clear Roman capitals that Susan and I prefer and the builders did the carving perfectly. As the same size (three inches high) and style of lettering would be suitable for her successor, we took a rubbing of the name (omitting the I of the IV) and Graham made a first-class job of carving it in three kauri boards, although I believe that was his first attempt at such work, and Ray, who traditionally gives a present to every boat built in his yard, paid for Graham's labour; he also gave the ship a teak cockpit grating.

Susan painted the bow nameboards green to match the green topstrake to which they would be secured, and as there was no gold leaf available she mixed yellow and orange paint until she had a fair imitation, and picked out the letters with that. The board for the stern she painted white, and did the letters in topstrake green so that they stood out well. Fortunately the law no longer called for a port of registry to be displayed, as this could have caused us some embarrassment; if we sailed about the south-west Pacific with Southampton on the stern people would be sure to ask when had we last left England, and although we had done so on four earlier occasions we would not have done so in this ship.

However, that nameboard on the stern had a special problem of its own. Graham fastened it correctly in position and none of us noticed anything odd about it until the yacht was afloat, when it had a curious downward curve as though looking into the water; this of course was caused by the combined rake and athwartships curve of the transom. The board looked so peculiar that we took it off with the idea of making a new one with a slight upward compensating curve; but this was beyond us, and eventually we screwed the original board to the after cockpit coaming which was flat; but there it was partly obscured by the taffrail and rudder stock.

*   *   *

'I name this ship *Wanderer V.*' Susan's voice, crisp and clear, rang out across the yard. 'May God bless her and all who sail in her.'

The christening bottle shattered on the anchor at the stem-head, pale wine sprayed over the bows, and eleven months after her lines had been laid down in the mould loft, and six weeks ahead of schedule, our new cruising home glided down the ways. When she reached the water and her heel lifted off the cradle her bow dropped for a moment so that she gave the impression of making a little curtsey to the assembled crowd, which in spite of the south-east gale and heavy rain was of considerable size and included the little black-and-white cat who had by now shifted her habitat from the hay barn to the big Herreshoff ketch next door, where the handouts were probably more generous and tasty.

Looking back on those eleven months of building, with the

countless decisions that had to be made, the compromises, the changes, as day by day a graceful yacht materialised from a pile of sweet-smelling timber and many gallons of pungent glue, I realised I had enjoyed them as much as any other period in my life, and I thought what a lot of interest, excitement and satisfaction is missed by those who buy a boat 'off the shelf' with everything already properly organised. But it had not been so much fun for Susan who had made herself responsible for the financial side of the business, and who so readily put aside whatever she was doing when I needed to discuss with her some practical matter that was worrying me. Our relations with the yard had been good, and if I ever need a reference I will quote what Ray said when he was interviewed by the press:

'There wouldn't be many owners you could have living in the yard for six months and still get on well, and Eric was in my office at 7.30 every morning. There is a generation gap too – I'm thirty-five and Eric is over seventy – but it never showed.'

From my vantage point aboard a hauled-out power yacht I watched as the launching crew started the engine to circle round and berth at the marina. I noted with relief that she was not after all down by the bows as I had feared in my more gloomy moments, but was floating nicely level fore and aft. With her springy sheer, broad, green topstrake and white spars, she was pleasing to my eye. When she turned her stern towards me I felt for a moment, as indeed I had all along, that it was a rather peculiar stern though not an unpleasing one (some people called it exotic) with its broad, curved transom steeply raked and topped by the open teak rail.

Wind and rain were playing havoc with the string of code flags with which someone had earlier dressed the ship. Every time the string parted another halyard was used to set it up, so that by evening when I went aboard to take in the ensign the ends of all three halyards were at the masthead. Not until morning did I get aloft (on the topping lift) to retrieve them and disentangle the wet, flapping bunting.

Meanwhile the drink and barbecued-sausage party, which Ray and Barbara had provided in the hay barn, was under way. There were many people whom I did not know, and when I asked Ray who they were he said he did not know them either.

Of course the yard employees had been invited with their families, but that could not account for the crowd; it appeared that anyone passing and hearing the party, which was making more and more noise as the beer and wine flowed, joined in. It was to continue well into the night.

For a week *Wanderers IV* and *V* lay side by side in the marina so that we could conveniently tranship our belongings from the one to the other, and it was noticeable as we did so that the big ship's waterline rose but the little one's did not go down as much as we had expected–apparently she was a good weight-carrier. Sadly we spent our last night in the 'manor house', as it were, before moving into the 'gardener's cottage', though a very nice cottage it was, and Stuart and Pam took possession; it was good to hand over the old ship to people we liked and respected. The last we were to see of her was some time later when by chance we met under way in the Bay of Islands; she looked very trim and was outward bound for Vila in Vanuatu at the start of the long trail to South Africa and beyond.

When the tide served we tried out our new ship under power. This was a fair success, which was surprising because not until it was over did we discover that while he was applying the second coat of anti-fouling paint, Chin had stuffed into the exhaust pipe a tightly rolled piece of rag to stop a trickle of water there, and had forgotten to remove it. Naturally this blockage disclosed the weakest part of the exhaust system, but that was soon put right.

However, there were some other matters that needed attention. When we took on fresh water for the first time alarming noises, like supersonic booms, came from each tank. The sole had to be taken up so that holding-down timbers could be fitted across the tank tops–a precaution too often neglected by many builders who believe tanks need support only at the bottom and sides–and the much-too-small air vent pipes, which misguidedly had been interconnected, had to be separated so that each tank could have its own. Nevertheless we still had occasional booms as the tanks 'oilcanned', and were concerned about it when a friend in Portugal wrote to tell us that aboard a yacht that he had had built in England to Lloyd's classification all the stainless steel tanks ruptured at the welds.

We consistently found a pool of water on the saloon table after heavy rain, and when we removed the central deckhead electric light fitting its bowl was found to be full of water; so the water must have been running along the gutter in the king plank where many of the wires, including those serving the mast lights, had been laid. It was not possible that there could be a leak in the cabin top deck, for that was of overlapping sheets of plywood glued together and coated with epoxy and dynel; therefore the only possible entry for the water must be at the mast-step. So the mast had to be lifted by crane, all concerned gathered round like surgeons at an operation, and sure enough it was found that the hole in the mast-step through which the wires passed had not been sealed, and rain trickling down inside the mast had crept along the wires. It was impossible to dry the gutter and wires, but we did take the opportunity to remove from the step the debris of alloy drillings, cuttings and welding that was found to be lying in it, and thereby eradicated one source of mysterious rattles.

With a metal mast which has no cap at its lower end it is hard to know where to place the sovereign which traditionally every good ship has under the heel of her main mast. I do not know why we did not glue it to the centre of the mast-step, where at least it would have been visible, though perhaps vulnerable, whenever the mast was lifted, but our golden coin finished up invisibly underneath the step, a place from which it can never be retrieved in case of urgent need – it must have increased greatly in value since it was minted – without first uprooting the step.

After several days of calm the wind returned, and with the sailmaker and rigger on board we set the sails for the first time. By our recent ketch standards we found our sloop close-winded, and in light conditions she sailed along at surprising speed, carried her way well when the wind fell lighter, and tacked with confidence even when headed just as she was going about. Later we were to discover that she had another virtue: she would work to windward and tack under the headsail only, which could be convenient when approaching a small harbour or crowded anchorage, for one could take in the mainsail before entering, work up to a berth under headsail alone, and then quickly roll the sail up with its furling gear.

So far we were very pleased with her, but when in the afternoon the wind freshened and she moved at five knots or more she was difficult to steer. When she was running it was almost as hard to force the tiller down as it was to force it up, and on a broad reach when she heeled to a strong puff she pulled so hard on the helm as to be almost unmanageable.

Our immediate reaction was that our fine new ship, on which we all had spent so much time and thought in planning, and loving care in building, was possessed of an unbalanced hull– that broad stern and comparatively fine bow?–a design fault that had been common enough in the past but which is rare today. When such a hull heels there is more body aft on the lee side requiring to be pushed down into the water than there is forward, and of course it cannot go, so the hull trims down a little by the head inducing weather helm. Whether the hull was unbalanced or not it was obvious that something must be done to ease the steering, and everyone concerned offered their views, most agreeing that the centre of effort of the sail plan should be moved further forward. There were several ways of achieving this: the roach could be trimmed off the mainsail, the rake of the mast could be reduced, the mast could be moved further forward, or a bowsprit could be fitted.

Alan the designer was in favour of moving the mast, but I would not sanction this. It was already far enough forward and if moved further might, by its weight, aggravate any tendency of the yacht to trim by the head; it might also reduce her ability to heave-to or lie a-hull properly in bad weather; besides, the hull had of course been stiffened and strengthened with frames, knees, floors and bulkheads at the mast's present position, and if the mast were to be moved those things would not be in the right place. Neither did I want a bowsprit unless we changed the rig from sloop to cutter, for in my view a mast should not rely for its total forward support on a stay leading to a projection from the hull; if the rig was changed both mast and rigging would need modifications, and two new headsails, jib and staysail, with new positions for their sheet leads, would be required.

We therefore accepted the first two options. Neale, almost

with tears in his eyes, took away the mainsail to cut off its roach and the rigger and I altered the rake of the mast by easing off the backstay and tightening the forestay.

Susan and I then went off for a short cruise on our own, and it soon became clear that the slight alterations to mast and sail had made no noticeable difference; the ship was just as difficult to steer as before, and the Aries vane gear, which had steered *Wanderer IV* so well, and which we had retained and fitted to the new yacht, could not control her except in light winds forward of the beam.

Since it was not just weather helm, but helm in either direction that was so hard to apply, Susan and I finally reached the conclusion that this must be due to the steep rake of the sternpost and rudder, in that much of the helmsman's effort was being used not in steering the ship, but in trying to drag her stern down into the water. Though there are of course many yachts with sternposts and rudders as steeply raked as ours was—folkboats, tumlaren, H 28s, etc.—their hulls do not possess the very wide stern we have, and which probably tends to trap aft-flowing water between it and the rudder. Nobody agreed with us, but we were convinced our diagnosis was right and were determined to have the angle changed.

For this to be done we returned to the yard and were hauled out stern-first so that without having to remove the mast our stern would be protected from the weather in an open-ended shed. Although the defect was in no way Ray's fault he treated us generously, made no charge for hauling us out, and let us have Graham Johnson to do the work with no yard mark-up for his labour. We got Graham to lengthen the keel by three feet and build a new sternpost with a rake of only 10° instead of 40°, and fill in the gap between with extra deadwood; inevitably this increased the wetted area by about 15 square feet. As the original rudder was now too long and narrow to be used again it was scrapped and a new one was built. Its stock now could not come up outside the transom, but passed instead through a rudder trunk which reached the deck three feet further forward; so the tiller now swept the cockpit although I had shortened it as much as I dared, and it caused much inconvenience. Wheel steering would have overcome this, but we were reluctant to spend any more money on alterations. The new arrangements are shown in dotted lines on the sail plan (Fig. 1).

We shared the shed with an old lifeboat whose owner was adding a deck and wheelhouse and converting her into a fishing vessel for the open waters east of Great Barrier Island. His favourite tool was a grinder which I believe he preferred to a saw, even for cutting sheets of plywood, and the noise at times was such that we who were continuing to live aboard could not converse; but neither could we complain, for if one chooses to live in a boatyard one has to share it with others no matter how much noise or mess they make. Besides, the fisherman was such a nice chap; we had met him some years before while cruising to the South Island when he was a top-dressing pilot, and he had been kind and hospitable.

After three weeks the work was finished, we were put back into the water, and as we started to motor down the narrow river we at once noticed a strange thing. The right-handed (clockwise turning when viewed from aft) propeller should of course tend to turn the bow to port when driving ahead, as indeed it had done before, but now the bow turned the other way, and a steady pull had to be kept on the tiller to stop the ship going off to starboard. We found that the bias to starboard was just the same when under sail as it was under power, and if the tiller was left free the ship would go off to starboard and turn in a circle and continue doing so until the helmsman took control again. However, to our great relief we found that the major and expensive operation she had just undergone was largely a success. The steering was greatly improved; she was steadier when running, and the vane gear was now able to control her in a wider range of conditions. Certainly she still pulled hard on the helm when heeled in a strong wind, but that was something we would have to learn to live with, and we noted that in a freshening wind we would need to reef the mainsail long before reducing the area of the headsail.

In early days with *Wanderer IV* we had a similar steering trouble, which was traced to a difference in curve of the sides of the rudder and was so slight that calipers were needed to detect it. This was corrected by fitting a small trim-tab to the trailing edge of the rudder. We supposed that something similar was the cause of our present steering defect and perhaps we might try a trim-tab again later on, but we certainly had no intention of returning to the yard and hauling out again now, and time was getting short if we were to leave New Zealand on our maiden voyage as planned in late April before winter set in.

PART III
Maiden Voyage

As Cape Brett, our point of departure from New Zealand, dropped astern the wind freshened and it was a splendid day on which to start a voyage. The sea was deep blue and white-capped under a cloudless sky; the easterly swell, though high enough to hide the land from us when we were in the trough, was gentle and the wind was fair. A variety of seabirds wheeled, glided, skimmed and dived around us, for those waters were full of life, and our new ship glistened as she hurried along under her tan sails, leaving a clean wake astern. For the first time Susan and I were able to listen to her deep-sea chorus. Aloft, the predominant note was a high-pitched whistle from the slits in the anti-chafe tubes on the shrouds, and some unfamiliar clanging of metal fittings on the alloy spars; the wood spars of our earlier yachts never made a noise like that. However these sounds did not drown the rumble of the bow-wave, the hiss of the wake, or the gurgle of the cockpit drains. As she rolled there came from below a wood-upon-wood creaking of the companionway steps, which I quickly silenced with strips of self-adhesive draught-excluding tape, and there were lovely contented chuckles as the water flowed swiftly along the smooth, wooden hull.

We were bound tentatively towards Tahiti, but as that island lay more than 2,000 miles away to the east-nor'east and headwinds could be expected, it might prove to be too much of an undertaking for us in our new and untried vessel.

Our feelings of excitement and pleasure were tinged with apprehension, for we had no idea how our ship would behave or her gear perform in heavy weather. Would she heave-to properly or lie a-hull? How would she behave when running before a gale and a steep following sea? Would her motion be easy or wild? Could her gear put up with the constant motion and wet conditions of an open-water passage and be free from wear and chafe? Of course we ought to have learnt more about her before leaving, but had been so occupied with preparations for the voyage and with the alterations that had to be made to her, that we had done no more than sail coastwise in moderate weather and smooth water and had not even spent a night at sea.

However, we were soon to have the answers to some of our queries, for that evening after the land had dropped below the horizon a bank of cloud came hurrying to cover the sky, and the wind increased. While there was still daylight we jointly took in the first reef and rolled up the jib. Then we set the staysail and at once found that the three-part tackle I had arranged for setting up the inner forestay was inadequate, and the little sail sagged away to leeward like a sack. Meanwhile the glass was falling and at 18.30 a gale was forecast.

It was some time after nightfall when the increasing wind called for the second reef, but now Susan could not help me as the wind-vane steering gear was overpowered, and she had to remain at the helm. As I struggled to take in the reef I wondered how I could have been so foolish as to have the old style pendant-and-point type of reefing with all its complications instead of the quick and simple roller gear to which I was accustomed. Of course I had tried out the arrangement, though only in smooth water and with not much weight in the wind, but now that I was doing it in earnest in rugged conditions in the dark, I discovered some of its shortcomings.

To hold the slugs in the mast-groove when the sail was lowered, a small pivoted stop engaging an invisible slot in the groove was provided. It was easy enough to lift this and let out the desired number of slugs for the reef, but groping in the dark trying to re-engage it occupied several frustrating minutes—a simple turnbutton would have been very much better. Later I made use of a lacing to hold the slugs to the eyelets in the sail, and then did not have to remove the slugs from the groove. Having pulled the reef cringle down to the boom I engaged it with the hook on the 'T' fitting at the gooseneck. This, too, was easy, but to hold it there while re-tensioning the luff with the halyard winch, which needed two hands, seemed almost beyond me. Since then several people have told me ways of holding the cringle on the T with plastic tube or elastic, but I believe a short length of rope made fast to the cringle and led through the tack cringle to a cleat on the boom would be simpler.

The reefing pendant was rove in traditional fashion, up from the boom, through the cringle on the leech, down through a sheave on the side of the boom, and forward to a winch; there was a winch for each reef. On this occasion the winch happened to be to leeward, and as I tried to work its handle with one hand and tail with the other I was pushed away and buffeted by the bag of wind-filled sail; it was quite a business to get that cringle down to the boom, and the fact that the sail got pinched between the two parts of the pendant did not help. Then the boom had to be hauled inboard so that I could reach and tie the reef points, for we do not belong to the school that is happy to sail with a big bag of sailcloth hanging under the boom ready to fill with spray or rain. In the days of hemp and manilla rope, as I recall, it was not all that difficult, but synthetic rope is too slippery for the purpose. Some time later we removed the points and used a lacing instead; we found this easier than tying points, but it needed the two of us to pass it, one to windward and the other to leeward. Finally I lashed the cringle to the boom as a precaution, and it was as well that I did so, for that second reef was to stay in for several days, and when we came to shake it out the pendant was found to be cut almost through where it had chafed on the sharp edge of the metal sheave-box, and without the lashing would surely have parted.

I had read in a chandler's catalogue that a 'jiffy' reef, as this method is sometimes called as though it were something new, can be taken in in 30 seconds. I wished the writer could have been with us that night to demonstrate, for it took me more than half an hour, but no doubt if I had had two or three people to help me, as in racing yachts, it could have been done more quickly. Then again some people lead the halyard and the reefing lines to winches aft, thus avoiding the need to leave the safety of the cockpit; but I would not be happy with such complications, and I would still want to tie the points. Although a sail reefed with roller gear may not set quite so well, for us that would be a small price to pay for the ease and speed of that method of reefing.

By the time I returned to the cockpit I was wet, tired and very cross with myself for going in for such an awkward and inefficient set-up, and Susan entirely agreed when I said that we must install roller gear as soon as possible.

But we were not finished with deck work yet, for the gale continued to increase, as did the sea. Loud above the other noises an occasional metallic clang disturbed us until we discovered that it came from the boom gallows, a massive affair consisting of two stainless steel pipes hinged to the cabin top, at their lower ends supporting a stout wood cross-member with notches in it to take the boom. It was lying on the cabin top, as it always did except when the mainsail was lowered, and when the ship dropped into a trough she did it so quickly that the gallows was left momentarily in mid-air only to fall with a crash a split second later. We lashed it down.

By midnight we were sailing too fast for our peace of mind and physical wellbeing, and as the wind was on the starboard quarter it aggravated the ship's insane determination to turn to starboard; so again the wind vane was overpowered, and steering by hand was hard and exhausting work. We therefore took the mainsail in and ran on at a more sedate speed under the staysail alone. That job should have been easy, for the mainsail was now only half its full size, but again it took too long—partly because without it the motion became wilder, making it difficult for us to hang on and at the same time make fast the gaskets, and partly because I had failed to engage properly that silly little gimmick intended to stop slugs from leaving the mast-groove, so all of them dropped out as the sail came down. We erected the gallows and got the boom safely on to it, and as the vane could now manage the steering we both went below, but failed to sleep because of the noise and the motion and a feeling of foreboding. I thought nostalgically of last night's smooth anchorage cradled by hills, and wished we were there instead of out in this turmoil.

The weather outlook was bad. The barograph was falling

steeply—it was to drop 35 mb (about 1 inch) in 36 hours—and the New Zealand news on the radio told of a deep depression with storm-force winds that had stopped the big Cook Strait ferries running for two days. The disturbance was said to be moving away to the north-east. This it did and we got the full benefit of it a little later when, having run for two days under staysail only, we had to take that sail in and continue under bare poles in Force 9. At some time during the third night the lifebuoy, together with its light, was torn away from its stowage on the guardrail and lost—fortunately it did not have our name painted on it—and all that remained to show where it had been was the little canvas bag in which its light had rested.

Our ship proved to be buoyant although heavily laden; she lifted quickly and easily to the overtaking seas, and seemed well able to take care of us in these conditions; but the violent wind, continuous heavy rain and crests on deck were showing up some weak points.

There was a bad leak at the galley skylight, which repeatedly soaked Susan as she struggled manfully to get us some simple, hot food. This was due not to poor workmanship but to the coaming being too low, and more than a week was to pass before it was dry enough to seal with masking tape. The staysail sheets had chafed badly at the deck fairleads because sharp ridges had been left when their bullseyes were turned; I tried with little success to smooth them with a file, and in the end lashed a spare block to each. When the sail was next used we knotted the sheets where they were chafed and turned them end-for-end. As the weathercloths which were rigged on the guardrails each side of the cockpit had been made a little too big we could not lash them taut, so their brass eyelets beat the stanchions and rail capping with a noise as of machine guns. This went on relentlessly day and night, and the lacings passing through them chafed and had to be renewed, after which some of the eyelets were torn out.

By the time we had sailed 300 miles on our way and were somewhere south of the Kermadec Islands, though not quite sure of our position because celestial navigation had been impossible, the wind, which had moderated a little but was still at gale force, backed steadily for four hours and settled in the east, i.e. dead in our teeth. The forecast, which was growing faint (we had not been able to find the short-wave station as we did not know its frequency) suggested this would continue. Clearly we were in no fit state to start trying to beat to windward in such weather, so with some reluctance, for we do not like to abandon a project once it has been started, we bore away and headed for much nearer Fiji which then was only about 1,000 miles distant (chart B). As it turned out we were to make most of that passage under the close-reefed mainsail and staysail, and sometimes under the latter alone; the whole jib was used for a total of no more than 12 hours throughout the following days.

More problems arose. Those sharp boxes for the reefing pendant sheaves chafed several holes in the mainsail, and the cloth was cut clean through as though by a knife at the upper batten pocket where it pressed against a shroud, because (as we discovered later) the plastic batten had a sharp backbone running its full length. In 30 years of voyaging this was the first time any sail of ours had been seriously damaged by chafe. Then one afternoon, in a rare quieter moment when we were both below, we heard a sharp tap on the cabin top; we clambered out on deck and found that this had been caused by one of the eight screws that held the goose-neck fitting to the mast falling out. Two others had already gone the same way, and the remainder were loose. Perhaps the whistle for 'smoke-o' blew just as someone was fitting them. Miraculously none of the screws had gone overboard and all were retrieved, one from inside the water-trap ventilator near the mast. I would have put them back with some adhesive, but there was too much rain and spray, so thereafter it was routine for one or other of us to go round every few hours with a screwdriver to check these and other screws. We carried a spanner as well for other things, such as the bolts holding the tiller at the rudder stock head and the hoops of the cockpit hood, were inclined to work loose with the constant motion.

There were some minor matters that called for attention: drawers that jammed because they had swollen with the pervasive damp, plastic door fasteners that could not withstand a 20° angle of heel, and chainplates that leaked into the

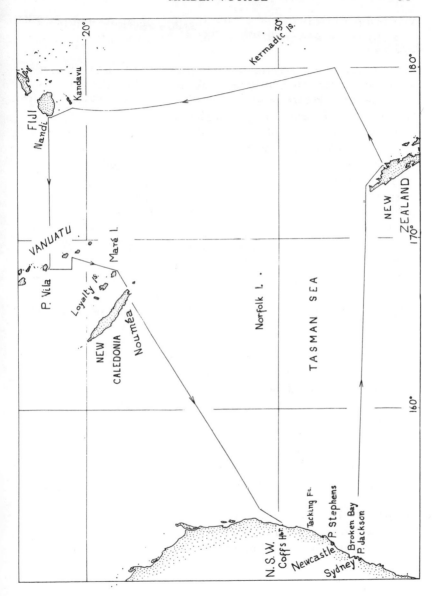

Chart B

wardrobe and the locker where our photographic equipment was stowed, but I could do nothing about the latter until we reached port.

However, a very serious thing happened one night when the ship was steering herself under staysail only and the vane gear was disengaged: a sea smashed the hinge casting of the gear and the servo blade was carried away and lost. This was a near disaster for we were no longer physically equipped to steer watch and watch for days on end, and for a little while we debated whether we should return to New Zealand or continue for Fiji. However, since it seemed no more difficult to go on than to retreat—for steering would probably be necessary most of the time either way—we decided to continue; besides, we believed the weather must surely improve as we made northing into the tropics. But it did not. The wind rarely dropped below Force 6 and was often at Force 7 or 8, and day after day there was low, damp cloud or rain. Then when the wind became more northerly to head us away to the west of the rhumb line we began to wonder if we would fail to make Fiji and find ourselves in New Caledonia instead; but mile by mile we managed to claw our wet way north.

Navigation was largely by dead reckoning, for the sun shone only occasionally, its woolly orb seen but briefly through fast-moving cloud, so I was fortunate in getting a couple of observations the day before we expected to make a landfall on the west end of Kandavu, the south-westernmost island of the Fiji Group.

After the way we had been treated by anti-British port officials on our last visit to Suva we would never go there again, so we had chosen Lautoka in Nandi Waters at the west end of Viti Levu, Fiji's largest island, as our port of entry, and the next afternoon when we had Kandavu on the beam the distance to go was 70 miles. As a low island lay only a few miles east of the direct course, and we did not wish to pass it in the dark because the light on it shone only over a northerly arc, we hove-to on the offshore tack before nearing the island and spent seven wonderful hours sleeping.

Letting draw at first light we passed the low island in the forenoon and by mid-day had sighted Viti Levu ahead. Still the cloud was low and damp and the wind, coming from more nearly aft now, increased again. We now had the whole badly damaged mainsail set for the first time in two weeks, for we were anxious to move as fast as possible and identify the leading beacons into, and find an anchorage in Nandi Waters before dark. We sailed faster than I could recall ever having sailed in a yacht with a waterline of less than 35 feet, for given the right conditions our new ship certainly had a good turn of speed.

Along that stretch of coast there is a fringing coral reef extending between $\frac{1}{4}$ and $1\frac{1}{4}$ miles from the shore; on it the ocean swell was breaking in a smother of pale-green and white with a chilling roar too clearly heard by us. Sometimes the breakers stood across our bows where a spur of the reef thrust seaward, and we had to steer with care and concentration to edge away, the more so as the steering defect was trying to turn us towards those fearsome breakers.

We made excellent time as the wind whistled in the rigging and the bow-wave roared, and still on the same gybe as we had been for the entire passage, we swept in through Navula Passage (the best of the passes into Nandi Waters for it is wide and straight), two hours before sunset, and suddenly found ourselves sailing in smooth dark-green water under a clear blue sky. Still at high speed we skirted a low, rounded headland where people were fossicking on the fringing reef, and with the hand lead, for the Mariner echo-sounder could not make up its electronic mind whether we were in two or twenty-five fathoms, sounded our way into a wide bay and let the anchor go on mud in six fathoms.

As the sun dropped to the horizon beyond the barrier reef the wind died away for the first time in 16 days and a faint offshore air brought out to us the aroma of wood smoke and sunbaked sugar cane.

*　　　*　　　*

In the past a visiting yacht arriving at a port of entry in a foreign country anchored with the international code flag 'Q' flying and waited for the port officials to come out and complete the necessary paperwork. Today, though, one is unlikely to know the correct procedure, which can vary from country to country and change from time to time even in the same place. In many ports the officials have no boat or radio and keep no lookout, and one might wait for days without anything happening. Sometimes one is expected to go ashore and seek out the officials, in others they are angry if this is done. Therefore on arrival now we usually ask some other yacht already there what the correct procedure is, and did so when we reached Lautoka.

'Anchor and go ashore by dinghy,' we were told. But the Indian official in the customs house was displeased. He said we should not have landed without permission and when I asked how we could have got permission he shook his head and told us to wait beside the dinghy for the man from the health department who would be summoned by telephone from some distant office. Half an hour later that official arrived and said he must go on board, so taking an oar each Susan and I rowed him off. He went below, looked at nothing, asked no questions, and made out the *certificate of pratique* at the saloon table. After we had put him ashore we had to repeat the operation with the customs official. He at least did something; he sealed up the few bottles of drink we had. I believe he enjoyed lolling in the stern of the dinghy and being rowed to and fro in the heat by a couple of oldies, but he did not say so, indeed he said very little except that he lived at Mba, was 21 years old and had two children.

We were to see a lot more of him, for each time we left Lautoka for some other anchorage in the area, even though it might only be a few miles away, he insisted that we obtain a clearance, just as though we were going foreign, and each time we returned we had to enter as though coming from another country. By the time we were ready to leave Fiji a pile of papers signed by us had accumulated in his office.

Lautoka is a sugar town. The mill is at the port with its own wharf where ships are loaded in bulk, and the cane is brought to it from the plantations by a network of narrow-gauge railways. The gleaming rails of one of these ran along the middle of the town's main street in an avenue of splendid trees, including many royal palms, and when one of the 100-truck-long trains was slowly passing through, its little diesel locomotive hooting importantly, much of the road traffic was brought to a halt.

Apart from this, the main street with its row of shops selling radios, watches, perfume and other items for the tourist, held little interest for us; but a much more useful street running parallel to it had many stores offering the things we needed, and it led to a very good market. Most of the shopkeepers and stallholders were Indian, and they rarely smiled, but such Fijians as we met and passed the time of day with, in particular the older ones, possessed the traditional Fijian air of courtesy, dignity, and a desire to be friendly and helpful. Some offered the opinion that Lautoka had been spoilt by too much road traffic, 'So small a place does not need all these cars. People should walk.'

As the anchorage at Lautoka was dirty with the soot and ash belched out from the seven chimneys of the sugar mill and had no good place at which to land and leave the dinghy, we investigated Sawene Bay, four miles down the coast. We would need to go to Lautoka now and then to collect mail and do some shopping, and presently to pick up the new blade for the vane gear which was to be flown out from England. If Sawene was alright we could travel to town by bus and such an arrangement would avoid the time-consuming business of entering and clearing.

We made our way there under power, for there was no wind that day, and pilotage was difficult because the water was so thick with silt that the reefs were invisible even where they had only a few inches of water over them. However, as we had arranged to arrive at low water, the two reefs guarding the inner anchorage were just awash, so we crept in between them and let the anchor go in two fathoms. However the place would be no good for us as a base if we could safely enter or leave only at low water—we failed to find any suitable landmark which would serve to lead us in or out on a compass bearing—and it was too open to the north, from which direction we knew the wind sometimes blew strongly.

We spent the night there and then sailed 20 miles to the south-west to the island of Malolo Lailai, which we had visited nine years before and knew it provided one of the best anchorages in Nandi Waters. As we left the mainland astern the water became clearer and the extensive reefs of the several small islands we passed on the way showed up well, as did the channel to the anchorage. This was just as well because the last hurricane had destroyed several of the beacons which used to mark it and Susan, standing on the boom to gain a little extra height of eye, conned us in without difficulty.

While weighing the anchor that morning there had been a little trouble with the windlass, the gipsy of which was binding on the chain stripper, so now we anchored temporarily with kedge and warp while I attended to it. When the yacht was a-building we had specified our ground tackle requirements precisely and supposed it would be a simple matter to obtain them, but there were difficulties. It was easy enough to get two genuine CQR anchors, one of 60 lb as the bower, and one of 45 lb as the kedge. We wanted 40 fathoms of $\frac{7}{16}$ in (11 mm) chain, but in New Zealand, like most other things, chain had gone metric and there was none available between 10 mm and 13 mm (approximately $\frac{3}{8}$ and $\frac{1}{2}$ in respectively). The former was a bit on the light side, and the other, which would weigh 300 lb more, too heavy to be carried as far forward as it would need to be, i.e. directly under the windlass. We therefore chose the 10 mm chain and subsequently regretted it, for in squally weather *Wanderer* sheered about considerably, and a heavier cable would have reduced that tendency which at times put a very heavy strain on the cable.

The only available electric windlass was a good-looking one with a chain gipsy to starboard and a barrel for rope to port. It had a powerful but very slow hand-operated back-up system for use in the event of an electric breakdown, or for breaking out the anchor when it was well dug in. Surprisingly the lever supplied did not fit either the hand gear or the brake/clutch, and we had to have one specially made. The switch was of the type that fitted flush into the deck and required a foot to be kept on it to keep the windlass working. That was no good, for if it were placed right forward so that one could stand on it and at the same time wash the chain as it was hove in, the switch would of course be out of reach when one wished to use the warping barrel. We therefore had a switch of the push-on, push-off type fitted on the windlass itself, and this called for a solenoid to be wired up below deck. When we came to weigh anchor for the first time we found that the windlass hauled in the cable much too fast so that it was impossible to wash it properly, and unless one hauled in short bursts the yacht gathered considerable headway, overran her anchor and was a danger to others lying nearby. The windlass therefore had to be returned to its makers for a different gearbox to be fitted at our expense.

The stemhead fitting, to my design, had two six inch diameter nylon rollers – their large size much reducing the waste of energy there – and the bower anchor stowed itself on the starboard roller with its shank inboard. The port roller was for use with the kedge. A Jabsco pump, belt-driven through its own clutch by the engine, sent sea water when required to a fitting on deck to which a hose was connected for washing the cable. Even so, mud might get below, and in order that this should not run right through the bilge to the bilge pump well, the cable stowed itself in a watertight, open-top box. Occasionally we let all the chain out and cleaned and dried the box with a swab.

It was a blessing to have ground tackle which was so easy to use and required no physical heaving or lifting, but naturally the windlass put a heavy drain on the batteries, so usually we had the engine running while weighing to provide some current and, of course, so that the cable-washing pump could be used.

I soon got the windlass to work properly again by adjusting the stripper, and we then anchored with bower and chain, but I did think, and not for the first time, what a pity it was that in New Zealand where they can and do build fine yachts with skill and loving care, so much of the locally made equipment was badly designed or of poor quality. I recalled that three lead/acid batteries had to be returned to the supplier because the specific gravity of the electrolyte differed from cell to cell, before we got a pair without defects.

Malolo Lailai, which was so small that one could walk round it, barefoot, on its sand beach in about an hour, had been bought by Dick Smith (an Australian) in 1966. He built two tourist complexes on it, the usual Fijian affairs, each consisting of a number of thatched *bures* for the guests to live in; there was a shop where they could buy food to cook for themselves, or they could eat gourmet meals in the central dining/drinking area.

The earlier establishment was called Plantation Village, and the more recent one, which Dick and his wife Carol were running, was known as Dick's Place. Between the two lay an airstrip through which, from our anchorage we could catch a glimpse of the mainland (the rest of the island being covered with palms) and to it a small plane came daily bringing provisions, visitors and mail.

On our earlier visit we had shared the anchorage with one other yacht; this time there were rarely less than ten and sometimes more than twenty with us – a small floating village. Of course the increase in numbers was largely due to the increased popularity of voyaging, but it was also because word had got round that Dick liked yachts and was generous and hospitable to their people. Not only did he let them have the run of the island, but he encouraged them to do their laundry ashore, using his water, and when pig was on the menu, roast in a pit, Fijian style, he often invited them to be his guests.

The inner anchorage was that precious thing, a secure berth with good holding ground and entirely free from moorings, but there was a rumour afoot that at least one 'yachtie' intended to lay a mooring for his own convenience. Unfortunately one mooring invites others, as we had often seen elsewhere, and in a short time a favoured anchorage can become cluttered with uninhabited yachts on moorings, and the would-be visitor must look elsewhere for a clear, safe place in which to drop his hook.

Most of our fellow villagers were from Australia, New Zealand and the U.S.A., but we did see Canadian and German flags, and no doubt there would be other nationalities when the annual west-bound voyaging fleet made its way across the South Pacific from Tahiti after *le Quatorze*. Some stayed only a night or two, others, like ourselves, remained for a month or more, and there were the almost permanent inhabitants – so far as voyaging people can be permanent in these immigration-conscious days – who had got into the habit of going there for six months (the longest period normally permitted) then sailing south to avoid the hurricane season and returning when that was over.

Near us lay the steel cutter *Si Ti Si III*. We first saw her American owners, John and Mary Lavery, in the Red Sea when they were making a circumnavigation in an earlier yacht. Some years later we met again in Hawaii where they were building houses to make some money, after which they had their present ship built in Tasmania. They made several fine voyages in the Western Pacific, and during a cruise the previous year among the Solomons they had the misfortune to strand by night on the windward side of a reef rising sheer out of deep water. Unable to get off by the same route as they got on, their only chance of survival was to drag the ship over the coral into the lagoon beyond. For several days they worked at this, laying out anchors by hand at low water and heaving on their cables at high tide, and inch by laborious inch they moved *Si Ti Si* with courage and determination until they achieved their objective. They sailed to New Zealand for a refit, where we met them again, and now here they were just as quiet and unassuming as ever. Their next port? Honiara. It seemed that in spite of their harrowing experience they were unable to keep away from the challenge of navigating in coral waters and unlike many of today's voyagers they carried neither ship/shore radio nor satellite navigation equipment.

Shortly after our arrival the Australian sloop *Cera* came in and her owners, Michael and Norma Henderson, introduced themselves as friends of a friend of ours. They were outward-bound from Sydney on a seven-year voyage, some parts of which would be against prevailing winds, but that would not be likely to bother them, for their ship was designed, built, and efficiently rigged for going to windward; for example, her shrouds came down not to the edge of the deck as ours did, but to the coamings of the coachroof, which had been strengthened with a steel girder, thus enabling the headsail to be sheeted well inboard, and her two pairs of crosstrees had been kept short for the same reason. Michael was a doctor, but he carried some metal-working tools and had the ability to use them, and he kindly moved the reef pendant sheaves along our alloy boom to positions where they should be more effective and less destructive to the sail. Norma—and how delighted we were when we learnt this—had been a professional sailmaker. She took our damaged mainsail away and not only repaired it superbly but improved it; she even folded it up, which is no easy thing to do aboard a yacht. As though all this was not kindness enough the Hendersons had us to dine in their immaculate, lamplit saloon, which like the rest of the accommodation had been built by Michael.

In coral waters some easy means of getting aloft to pilot by eye is desirable, and the more old-fashioned of us used to rattle down the lower shrouds for this purpose; but ratlines are hard on bare feet and take one only to the crosstrees. Then came mast stairs, little metal brackets screwed to a wood mast or riveted to one of metal; these, though comfortable enough, have the drawback of permanent weight and windage aloft, and it is not always possible to lead the running rigging clear of them. So for *Cera* the Hendersons had made a rope ladder with wood rungs; when required its lower end was secured to deck fittings just forward of the mast, and it was hoisted and set taut by a masthead halyard and a winch.

One of the more permanent inhabitants of our village was the cutter *Moira*. Richard, her owner, was a marine biologist, and one of his projects while at Malolo was to make what perhaps might be called a colour 'movie' of a rare coral on the reef close by. Each day he swam over this special feature and took one flashlight picture, so that when the series was completed and assembled he would have a chronological record of the growth of that coral. He was American, his charming mate, Freddie, was French/Moroccan. She too was busy, and one of her arts was the decoration of T-shirts. Since she and Richard were dedicated ecologists, much concerned at the slaughter of sea mammals, one of her shirt slogans read 'Save a whale, eat a Jap.' When they made their shopping expeditions to Lautoka, Freddie always brought us some little thing from the Indian market, a pineapple, bananas, a cabbage.

Another fully occupied and artistic couple lived aboard the sloop *Dragon*. Louis did scrimshaw on highly-polished whales' teeth (I wondered what Richard and Freddie thought of that) and his wife George (two women with male names in the same anchorage was unusual) painted highly professional portraits and cooked exotic dishes; indeed the dinner we were invited to aboard *Dragon* was so splendid and of such variety that we never had the courage to ask Louis and George to share one of our simple and unrefrigerated meals.

In Orams' marina while *Wanderer* was being built we came upon the elderly woodcutter *Fleetwood*. Her owners, Randy and Jamie Brown, had sailed her out from San Diego and were giving the handsome old yacht a loving refit. Now she lay close by and when visiting her we much admired the things that they had done; their varnishwork, for example, had the rich, smooth patina of French polish and put our own efforts to shame. A few days later they got their clearance for Vila and set out, but finding the wind blowing at 40 knots outside and a heavy sea running, they wisely put back to wait for an improvement. I think that had this happened to Susan and me we would have been restless, on edge, the more so as it is forbidden to stop at an out-island after obtaining a clearance from Fiji. But in the evening as the sun set in a threatening, bruise-like manner and the wind died away for the first time in many days, it was a pleasure to see Randy and Jamie relax in their bean-filled chairs (plastic beans, of course, as real ones would have been too heavy and likely to germinate) on *Fleetwood*'s cabin top, one each side of the boom, with drinks in hand.

The Americans were great at organising barbecues on the deserted beach at the north end of the island and invariably invited us to join them. But I never did enjoy picnics with sand in the sandwiches, and having participated in one of those barbecues I did not want to do so again. Chewing charred but underdone meat in almost total darkness while perched on a fallen palm and being eaten by mosquitoes seemed a poor substitute for a properly cooked meal eaten at a clean table in a good light and with all the bugs excluded, as in *Cera*. I sincerely hoped I would never become a castaway.

But our stay at Malolo was an enjoyable and busy one. We had brought a supply of wood and other materials with us, and having most of the tools we needed were able to make improvements and additions to our new ship and put right some of the defects that had come to light on the passage north. Among the things that Susan made were a windsail, cockpit awning and windlass cover; she repaired the weathercloths and altered them to fit, and when the weather served she rubbed down and varnished all the brightwork. With battens bedded and screwed, I turned much of the cabin top into a rain catchment, and there was such a lot of rain that winter that we did not have to take any water from the shore for the next four months. I managed to make the galley skylight watertight, and stopped (though only temporarily as I was to discover later) the tiresome leaks at the chainplates. Originally we had a winch on one of the cockpit coamings to handle the jib furling/reefing line, but having found that it was just as easy, and a good deal quicker, to work that line by hand, I removed the winch to the foredeck so that it could be used for setting up the inner forestay. I made a massive wood bracket so that the compass could be moved off the bridgedeck, where it was much in the way, to a position on the bulkhead, and . . . But anyone who has ever owned and sailed a new one-off cruising yacht will understand well how much there was to do, and that even now, a year later, we still have not finished, and therein lies much of the fascination of our way of life.

Most days we landed to walk on the island, bathed in the clean warm water that was like a caress and slept soundly once we had got into the habit of shipping the insect screens, for even out at the anchorage there were plenty of mosquitoes at night. I had made screen frames for all openings—hatches, skylights, ports—out of welding rod, and Susan sewed the netting on. They were light, cheap and easy to make and required little stowage space.

We made a couple of sorties to Lautoka to collect the new blade for the wind vane gear and to do more extensive shopping for food than was possible in Dick's little store, and always returned with pleasure and relief. But, like everyone else, we had to leave eventually to get on with our voyage and it was with nostalgia that we wondered where, if ever, we would again meet our friends from Malolo's floating village. Of course our berths would be taken by new arrivals, each to enjoy for a spell the pleasures and comforts of that good lagoon and the meetings with their neighbours until they, too, had to move on.

*   *   *

Under the low, grey sky the atmosphere was humid and salt, and above the beat of the rain and the deep note of a great wind in the rigging could be heard the hollow boom of seas breaking against the massive walls that protected us and the frequent hiss and rattle as showers of spray drove over them to invade the harbour and our deck.

For many years there had been a long wooden jetty there to serve the timber trade, but it was exposed, and in 1919 the Australian Public Works Department built Coffs Harbour round it, joining two small islands to the mainland with rock and concrete walls, but sensibly leaving the sand beach clear for the swell to expend itself upon. Unfortunately the stevedores' union killed the timber trade, so the decaying jetty lay abandoned and the harbour was used only by fishing vessels and yachts; for their protection inner walls with a narrow entrance between them had been built to give extra shelter from sea and swell and to allow a marina with a hundred berths to be established. In some respects that marina was unique: there was no water or electricity laid on, no lighting, and access was by a single-lane road along the top of the wall, which in very bad weather could not be used because of seas breaking over it. As the harbour thrust out from the shore into the Pacific those using it experienced the forces of Nature at first hand just as they would if at sea, except that they lay in safety in almost smooth water. Surprisingly little swell ran in, but there was often a surge which was hard on fenders and lines.

Susan and I were thankful indeed to be tucked up in there instead of being out in the grey, misty, white-capped wilderness of the ocean, at which we could look smugly from the top of the nearest wall, for the southerly gale then blowing was the third in ten days. But it was not only along the coast of New South Wales that the weather was unusual, for that winter—and winter is the time for cruising in the South-west Pacific because the summer months are subject to cyclones—had been remarkable for its bad weather, and few could remember a worse one.

Even in Nandi Waters at the usually quiet and dry west end of the Fijis, where we had spent two months, there had been a lot of rain and the trade wind often blew much too hard. However, the weather appeared to have improved when the time came for us to leave on the 550-mile passage from there to Port Vila in Vanuatu. That country, which comprises a chain of forty islands spread over seven degrees of latitude, had been until the previous year the British/French Condominion of New Hebrides, and we had heard conflicting reports on the outcome of independence.

The passage, one that we had made in the past in *Wanderer IV*, should have been a pleasant run in fine weather before a moderate trade wind, and we had been looking forward to it, but as Fiji faded out of sight astern the wind freshened and it continued to do so; bit by bit we reduced sail until we were under the close-reefed main and staysail, and the rising sea began to fling us about.

Being on the third day a little north of the rhumb line, two vigias lay ahead: 'Disc'd water rep'd 1944' and 'Shoal rep't 1965'—most of the dates given alongside such items on Pacific charts are earlier than that. From our angle of approach the channel between them was barely eight miles wide, so as the only thing reasonably certain about a vigia is that it is not where the chart shows it to be, we altered course to pass well south of their marked positions.

Towards the end of the passage we ran under the staysail only to reduce speed, and for the final 30 hours lay a-hull waiting for the sun to peep out through the dense cloud cover and allow us to fix our position before running in among the islands, for if we were to overshoot them it would be difficult, perhaps impossible, to beat back. As a result of this delay the passage took six days, but fortunately we managed to arrive on a Friday afternoon just in time for the port officials to deal with us before they knocked off for the weekend. They were polite but very serious as they painstakingly completed many forms, and one of them, after studying my passport, told me sternly that I ought not to be sailing at my age.

The waterfront had been tidied up since our last visit, and some of the 53 overseas yachts in port lay end-on to it, but we preferred to anchor in a less public and more sheltered spot inside Iririki Island, just off the empty but still well-maintained house that had been the British Residency, and go ashore by dinghy. The only disadvantage of that berth was that when the occasional tanker came with fuel for the island, all yachts had to move elsewhere until she had discharged her cargo, as though

The new ship sailing in New Zealand's Bay of Islands.

ABOVE LEFT At Port Vila we chose a sheltered berth in the lee of Iririki Island

ABOVE RIGHT A recent addition to the sad array of wrecks on New Caledonia's reef.

In smooth water with the vane gear steering on a broad reach; we had almost forgotten that sailing could be so enjoyable.

Coffs Harbour, made by joining two small islands to the mainland, thrusts boldly out into the Pacific.

Smiles of relief and satisfaction after the steering metamorphosis. From left to right, Hank, Joe and Susan.

Only two miles from the centre of Sydney, yet our berth Cammeray was flanked by native bush.

As we sailed up Sydney harbour, *Canberra* – recently returned to the tourist trade from the Falklands war – appeared beyond the opera house.

she carried some contagious disease.

The little town appeared to be much the same as in the past and still had a pleasant French flavour; the vendors in the open-air market on the waterfront under the casuarina trees still sat on the ground with their fruit, vegetables and shells spread out around them; the same shop displayed the same 'duty free' goods at the normal retail prices, and there was a plentiful supply of long, crusty loaves and *croissants*, and the biggest and best brown eggs that we had seen for a long time. There was something very likeable about the people, heavy-featured and toothless though many of them were, and they displayed a friendly and helpful attitude; each time we landed on the little sand beach opposite our anchorage people would come running to help us drag the dinghy up above high-water mark, and smiled shyly at our thanks. Although there were many young men standing about in the town seemingly with nothing much to do (it was said that they got the women to do the work and knocked them about if they didn't) they looked well-fed and healthy and most were dressed in clean, often brilliantly coloured clothes.

For the first two weeks of our stay the sky was heavily overcast and there was almost continuous drizzle or rain, and when eventually the sky did clear, the trade wind, which at that time of year normally blows at Force 4 or 5, blew with such vigour day after day that the fully-powered inter-island trading vessels bound south were able to make only two or three knots headway against it, and reported that the sea was 'rough to very rough'. Port Vila radio station was supposed to broadcast a weather forecast after the midday news (except on Saturday and Sunday when it did not broadcast anything), but as the news had to be read in three languages, English, French and Bislama (a kind of pidgin) there was often not time enough left for the weather, so sometimes of an afternoon we walked up the hill to the friendly meteorological office to get a forecast, but received no encouragement to sail.

There was much convivial sociality among the yachties who were growing impatient at the delay caused by the long spell of bad weather. Some, much concerned about navigating when the sky was so often overcast for long periods, had ordered satnavs from their home countries, and obviously could not sail until they arrived–they were still waiting for them when we left. One of the yachts that did leave when she intended to was the Australian cutter *Arriba*. Tony and his wife had built their fine vessel themselves of wood, and among many other trips had made an anti-clockwise circumnavigation of Australia, during which they had two remarkable experiences. While Tony was rowing the dinghy in a Queensland river where the yacht was anchored, his wife, who was sitting in the stern, was bitten in the back by a crocodile–crocodiles were a protected species and might not be shot without permission. We asked if she suffered any ill-effects such as blood poisoning, and it seemed not, but with a broad grin Tony told us that the reptile's saliva took the enamel off the dinghy just like paint-remover. The other incident was a dismasting in the Australian Bight, but they took that in their stride and nonchalantly told us that they just set up a jury rig and sailed to Adelaide.

One evening we attended a 'sardine' party (a real crush) aboard one of the fleet of yachts that had sailed north from New Zealand; the crews of most of them were there and the conversation was largely concerned with radio communications. It appeared that few of those present felt at ease when at sea unless they were able to speak with the other yachts several times a day about the weather, navigation, the port they were heading for, or exchange cooking recipes and all manner of gossip. We understood that even we, who had no transceiver, were discussed. Someone had broadcast our day of departure from Fiji and said which way we had been heading, so it was possible that anxiety might have been felt if we had not arrived within a reasonable time, and conceivably some search or enquiry might have been set in motion–meanwhile we could have changed our minds and our course and gone somewhere else.

As we rowed in the dark back to *Wanderer* I said to Susan that I felt our evening companions were missing something of importance: the wonderful satisfaction that could be theirs if they were to depend more upon themselves and their abilities while making a passage instead of discussing everything with others, just as they might by telephone while living in suburbia.

On arrival in a strange port they did not enjoy, as we did, the excitement and pleasure of exploring for themselves, for someone by radio would have told them where to anchor, which was the best store or hotel, that there would be 'happy hour' aboard *Mary Jane* tomorrow at six, and on Wednesday an expedition by bus to see the sights. Sometimes the people who were so dependent on radio even got themselves talked into a port instead of using their own commonsense and skill in pilotage, and occasionally with unpleasant results. The crew aboard one yacht that was being talked into Vila found themselves among reefs as they came in by night, yet the pair of red leading lights that would have brought them safely to the anchorage were burning brightly.

Susan agreed with me, but she pointed out that today nearly everyone does have radio, and if they wish to use it for such purposes that is entirely their concern. Of course it is, but it is the use of radio in calling for assistance without valid reason that most disturbs me, for any air/sea search that gets wide publicity, and most of them do, gives the rest of the sailing community an unjustly bad image and hastens the day when there will be wider legislation to curtail their freedom. For the most part it is yachts of racing type that cause the concern, not the thousands of genuine cruising/voyaging yachts that go quietly and efficiently on their way without bothering anyone.

Some little while after we had returned to New Zealand at the end of this Pacific cruise, yachts that had taken part in the Auckland to Suva race were sailing home and an easterly gale of 60 knots, which blew for about three days, caught some of them towards the end of the passage. We were at anchor in a well-sheltered cove at the time, and the only warning of this violent gale had been the appearance of the sky two days before it arrived; the sky was a tangle of continually fast-moving wisps of cirrus, and the sun had a halo. Remarkably, the barometer was very high, 1030 mb (30.4 in), and it did not begin to fall until the gale had started, nor had the radio forecasts given any warnings before then.

The following note on the events of that gale is not intended as stricture, for one has no right to criticise unless one was present or has entirely reliable details, but it may serve as a précis.

Yacht *A*, somewhere in the vicinity of Norfolk Island, radioed that she was sinking. An Orion of the R.N.Z.A.F. homed in on her emergency-position-indicating radio beacon and directed a merchant ship to her aid. All but one of the yacht's crew got aboard, the exception fell between ship and yacht and was crushed. With outstanding courage an officer dived from his ship's upper deck but failed to save the man. In order that the abandoned yacht should not be a hazard for others, she was scuttled. One therefore wonders if she really was in a sinking condition (photographs taken from the air did not show her to be), and had her crew not called for help might they not by their own efforts have brought her safely to port without losing one of their number?

Yacht *B* radioed for help as she had struck a rock. A frigate towed her in, but she too cannot have been mortally injured or she would not have survived the long tow in the heavy sea then running.

Yacht *C* called for help as she had 'rolled twice'; yet, escorted by the navy, she made port with only moral support.

Yacht *D* said that she did not know her position, which with torrential rain reducing visibility was not surprising. Perhaps she could have hove-to until able to get a fix, but again the navy helped.

Yacht *E* was wrecked on the coast about midnight at the height of the gale, and seven of her crew of eight were drowned. She had satnav, so should have known at the last satellite pass that she was standing into danger, and could have remained at sea on the offshore tack instead of continuing to head for the land. It was said that her owner, who was not on board, was in touch with her at the time by radio.

From this it would appear that three, if not four, of the five yachts should have caused no concern had they not called for help, then no air/sea search, no tow and no escort would have been needed. It also seems that some skippers are not prepared to stop and wait for conditions to improve, though it should be said that some modern yachts cannot be made to heave-to or lie a-hull safely.

Our intention on leaving Vila was to go to Noumea on the south-west side of the big French island of New Caledonia. To reach it we would need to sail south for 220 miles against the prevailing wind, round Ile Maré (southernmost of the Loyalty Group) and on another 70 miles in a south-west direction to reach Havannah Passage. This leads through the barrier reef, which is the second largest in the world, into the lagoon and round the southern tip of the island. Strong currents of uncertain direction can be met with between Ile Maré and the passage. *Pacific Islands Pilot,* Volume II, notes that vessels hove-to in that area at nightfall have drifted as many as 25 miles south-eastward during the hours of darkness, and others the same distance in a north-easterly direction, and in the passage the tidal streams attain a speed of five knots. As the passage was lighted we would plan to approach it shortly before dawn so as to have the benefit of the lights to fix our position (a common practice of yachts crossing the English Channel) and daylight for the final pilotage. To get the tide right it would be best to arrive at about full moon, and if time permitted we would stop at one or more of the islands on the way to Maré.

With all this in mind we obtained our clearance and left Port Vila the following day, but when clear of the harbour we found the headwind so strong and the sea so rough that we could make no worthwhile progress and returned to our anchorage. A second attempt two days later was also abortive, and not until a week had elapsed since getting our clearance did we finally get away. The port officials were understanding about this and said, 'No problem, we'll just re-date your papers.' However, the delay meant that we would have to make the passage direct.

The wind, though still ahead, had moderated as we beat slowly south past the islands of Eromanga and Tana, and in the late afternoon of the third day out of Vila we rounded the southern point of Ile Maré. The flat, featureless island looked sinister, *contra jour* as it was and with spume from the breaking swell rising like smoke against it.

Now we could ease sheets and cover the remaining distance comfortably before dawn; but as *Wanderer* was launched in torrents of rain and a south-east gale, and unsuitable weather had been her portion ever since, it came as no great surprise when very soon the wind died right away. To hold to our plan we therefore motored through the night; but when we had, by log, run our distance there was not a light to be seen and, fearing that a current might have set us south of the course and placed us close to the reef, we stopped and had breakfast while waiting for dawn. We then discovered by cross-bearings of distant headlands that the current had been setting not athwart our course but back along it, and that the nearest light with a range of 12 miles was still 17 miles away, so of course we had not seen it.

As the calm continued we motored on, and in time identified the leading beacons, which were squat and hard to pick up in daylight, swept into Havannah Passage with the fair tide hurrying us along, and on the very last drain of it entered Baie du Prony. Our old Admiralty chart of this was strangely misleading, but we found a perfect anchorage just large enough for one in a tiny unnamed cove, the shore of which was a tangle of mangroves, and the steep slopes above densely clad in bush and trees through which a small stream came chuckling down; apart from that only the voices of birds broke the silence.

On arrival at Noumea next day we found big changes had taken place since our last visit eight years before. As at Vila, the waterfront had been tidied up and reclamation works completed. The yacht club marina had increased in size and a commercial marina had been built adjoining it. Both appeared to be full, but that did not concern us as we preferred to lie at anchor head to wind, and no sooner had we brought up than our voyaging friends Michel and Jane de Ridder from nearby *Magic Dragon* came alongside with a welcoming gift of crusty new bread and fruit, and a little while later kindly collected the port officials and ferried them off.

We remained for two weeks of almost perfect weather and looking seaward through the harbour entrance we could watch the clear sun drop below the horizon, and four consecutive evenings saw it do so with a brilliant green flash; this, though common enough, is still one of the wonders of the tropics, yet surprisingly few people watch for it. Ashore there was little evidence to support the local belief that a bloody civil war would soon break out, but of course the casual visitor cannot see far below the surface. Getting about on foot in the traffic-congested town with its maze of one-way streets was no pleasure, but Susan was able to do her simpler shopping in a Chinese store close to our anchorage. The first time she went there she landed at the commercial marina and explained to the French custodian that she was from the English yacht out there and would like to leave the dinghy for a short time. He answered with what appeared to be a hostile torrent of French, little of which could she understand. When the de Ridders heard about this they asked the custodian what the trouble was, and he said, 'But she is English, and we can't have the English here; look what they did in the New Hebrides.' He was a volatile individual and one evening, when the owners of a yacht at his marina had invited friends to come for a drink, he forced the guests to lie on the ground and held them there at gunpoint until their hosts arrived. Thereafter Susan preferred to land on the beach.

Although our official entry at Noumea had been quick and easy, obtaining a clearance was another matter. We had to visit three widely-separated offices, immigration, customs, port; this business took us two and a half hours and involved a walk of nearly three miles.

Many vessels have ended their days on the great reef which encircles and projects 40 miles south of New Caledonia, and the rusting remains of several of them stood up sharp and clear as an awful warning to others. A recent addition to that sad array had been a large, schooner-rigged yacht; while attempting to enter the pass by night she must have misinterpreted the excellent lights, for she lay on her bilge with the swell breaking round her only about a mile from the great white tower with its 16-mile light standing on Ilot Amédée just inside the reef. It was from there that we took our departure to head south-west for Coffs Harbour on the east coast of Australia, some 850 miles distant.

The day was perfect as we slipped along at eight knots on a broad reach under full sail with the vane gear steering. The sea was remarkably smooth and we had almost forgotten that sailing could be so enjoyable; we wished we could have more of it, but in waters south of the Tropic of Capricorn one can never be sure of conditions remaining the same for long, and so it was on that occasion. After that first lovely day the wind became variable both in strength and direction, sometimes blowing at five knots, sometimes at twenty-five; it might be dead ahead one day, and on the next dead astern and not strong enough to keep the sails from slamming as we rolled in the swell. Three nights in a row it died right away, so we both turned in and slept; as a result progress was slow, and on only three days did we make runs exceeding 100 miles.

As on other passages in recent years, we found the ocean sadly lacking in wildlife. As pollution becomes more widespread (though we had seen little of it we were well aware of what had been happening elsewhere) and commercial fishermen employ larger vessels with more sophisticated gear, there are fewer creatures to be seen, except in higher latitudes. Occasionally one may have a visit from a handful of porpoises instead of the scores seen on earlier voyages, a solitary bosun bird perhaps, and a pair of cape pigeons; with luck one might sight a whale or two (we were fortunate to come upon a pod of small black ones that trip); only three flying fish came aboard where in earlier days there might have been a dozen or more on deck in the morning; and what, we wondered, had become of the little stormy petrels of which there used always to be some in sight in nearly every part of every ocean—we had seen hardly any since we were off the Canadian coast. However, we did come across some 'noddies' fishing near Capel Bank, and one of them (at least we supposed it was the same one, though they all look much alike) spent two consecutive nights on board, the first perched on the outboard motor, which was clamped to the pushpit mercifully to leeward, and the second on the windward guardrail beside the cockpit, leaving an astonishing quantity of droppings to be cleared up in the morning. These birds exhibit a remarkable ability to balance against a yacht's motion with head tucked under wing, and appear to be unafraid of man; when one on the foredeck seemed unwilling or unable to take off, Susan lifted it gently and held it head to wind; it made no protest, but spread its wings, circled round and alighted close beside her. Out of sight of land we saw only one vessel, an oriental fisherman.

During the eighth night out, when we were within 100 miles

of the Australian coast, Susan called me from my watch below to say that it looked as though a southerly buster was approaching; sure enough, low above the southern horizon was spread the unmistakable roll of cloud which often presages this Australian east coast phenomenon. We already had one reef in the mainsail and knowing that a buster brings a sudden change in wind speed and direction, we rolled up all of the jib and waited for it to arrive.

It will have been noticed earlier that for a strong wind, or in expectation of one, we were in the habit of rolling up the jib. This was because we regarded the roller gear, which was a new thing for us, as being fragile. We had seen that when the sail was partly rolled up its leech and foot imposed considerable bending strains on the alloy foil at the points where they came to it. Also, we believed that a weakness lay in the furling/reefing line. This had to be large enough to haul on by hand, but so that there should be a sufficient number of turns of it round the drum when the sail was fully set, the inner heart of that plaited kevlar rope had been removed to reduce the rope's diameter for the length that the drum would have to accommodate, thus much reducing its strength. This had been done in accordance with the instructions in the maker's handbook. On both counts I now believe we were wrong to mistrust the gear which had been designed and built to withstand the forces to which it would be subject in daily use at sea. But apart from this we believed, and still do, that the little storm staysail is a more seamanlike thing to use in heavy weather, and it had the great advantage that its centre of energy was well inboard, whereas the centre of energy of the jib moved further and further forward as the sail was increasingly reefed.

The management of yachts in heavy weather is largely a matter of opinion, yet much depends on the yacht herself, on her rig, her windage, and particularly on the shape of her underwater profile. The options are to heave-to under sail, lie a-hull, run before it, or lie to a sea-anchor.

Putting it briefly, to heave-to is to arrange the sail or sails and the helm in such a way that they counteract one another, so that the yacht lies almost stationary with the wind about 50° off the bow, i.e. in the closehauled attitude. She will probably fore-reach slowly and make a lot of leeway, resulting in a square drift, i.e. a general movement at right angles to the wind, but the less she moves the better. This is the safest action to take in the event of being caught by a gale off a lee shore. To get the yacht to lie a-hull all sail is taken in and the tiller is lashed to leeward; she should then lie stationary (except for leeway) beam-on to wind and sea; should she bear away and gather headway the lee helm will bring her back until again she lies beam-on. This is the simplest of all heavy-weather procedures and it calls for the minimum exertion on the part of the crew; it also has the merit that as the yacht drifts slowly straight down wind she will leave a slick to windward which will have a remarkably calming effect on the advancing seas. In that attitude, however, presenting her broadside to windward, she will become highly vulnerable should she move out from the protecting slick; in addition her motion will be more violent than if hove-to under sail. However, in the 30-foot sloop *Wanderer III* we lay a-hull on many occasions, and at no time was dangerously heavy water shipped.

If the gale happens to be blowing in the direction one wishes to go (provided this does not lead towards reefs or shore), running before it under much reduced sail, or perhaps under bare poles, will be the obvious action to take; it is good for morale, while lying stopped is not. We ran before several hard blows on the passage north to Fiji; we also did so in the 49-foot ketch *Wanderer IV* on a number of occasions. However, steering while running in heavy weather can quickly become exhausting, and the yacht may be in danger if she runs too fast, for then she will remain too long on the face of each overtaking sea, will become wild on the helm, and may broach-to, i.e. swing round broadside-on and perhaps be swept by a sea or even rolled over. Long ropes, and plenty of them, could then be streamed out from the stern in an attempt to slow her to a safer speed, but if they do not succeed a sea-anchor of the traditional type—a conical canvas bag with its mouth held open by crossbars or a metal hoop—might be used, and it will be effective provided it is big enough and strong. It is commonly thought that a sea-anchor of that type, if streamed from the bow, will hold a yacht head to wind; it is unlikely to do so, but if it did the yacht would be making sternway and a great strain would be placed on the rudder and its hangings. In *Wanderer III* we streamed a sea-anchor from the stern on two occasions, and it was satisfactory in reducing her speed to about one knot. It is said that the parachute type of sea-anchor will hold a yacht head to wind when streamed from the bow; I imagine its large area of light material might be difficult to control and launch in gale conditions, but I have had no experience with it.

We had yet to discover how our new vessel would behave when lying hove-to or a-hull, but were not to remain in doubt for long, as the wind soon backed swiftly from north-west to south with a sharp drop in temperature, and increased to 30 knots. We lashed the helm down about 20° so that *Wanderer* lay under the single-reefed mainsail and made slow progress in a westerly direction. However, as she was inclined to bear away too much before the helm checked her, we re-lashed the tiller as far over as it would go (about 35°) and left her to manage as best she could while we went below out of the rain.

Instead of blowing itself out after an hour or two, as busters usually do, that one went on and on and worked itself up into something rather special, but did not reach its peak until the following night when it exceeded 60 knots (violent storm, Force 11). But long before it attained such fury we had taken in the second reef, thus reducing the sail to about half of its full area.

Three hours after nightfall the wind suddenly started making a great commotion, howling (not whistling) in the rigging and heeling us steeply. The ship began to move too fast, bringing heavy water on deck; she ranged about unsteadily, now with wind abeam, now luffing, and when she luffed the sail and mast vibrated savagely and the whole ship trembled. Of course the sail should have been taken in earlier, but we had been scared of attempting it and had delayed, hoping the wind might moderate. But now the sail had to be handed at once, for if we delayed any longer it would surely carry away or do itself a serious injury.

After we had struggled into our foul-weather gear and our harnesses, which normally we did not use but felt we should wear now, we sat for a few moments discussing how best to tackle the job and which part each of us would play, for such was the noise on deck that we knew we would not be able to communicate by voice out there; then we slid back the hatch and clambered out. In the light of the nearly full moon the sea was a remarkable sight; as far as one could see it was covered with long streaks of foam, and spray was being driven horizontally from the crests—we had seen nothing like it since making our last rounding of Cape Agulhas. Because of the roaring wind we could move about, but with some difficulty and only on hands and knees; the simplest action was a hard struggle and our unaccustomed harnesses were a constant hindrance.

When we let the halyard go and clawed the thrashing sail down it bellied out to leeward but came down more readily than we had expected, the reason being that all the shoddy little plastic slugs holding luff to mast had broken, just as though a zip-fastener had been undone. Fortunately, though, there was a stainless steel slug at the headboard and lower down two others that Susan had seized on in anticipation of such a happening. As tiers could not hold the furled sail against the wind, which worried at every crease and pocket, we bound it to the boom with rope from end to end. Then we erected the gallows, but when we tried to get the boom down on to it, the moment the topping lift was eased only a trifle the heavy spar slammed from side to side; so we left it as it was, but in gloomy anticipation of the topping lift carrying away we backed it up with the main halyard.

With the helm still lashed hard down the ship was now lying a-hull, but not too well, for instead of keeping the wind on her beam she often turned her quarter to it so that she gathered headway and ranged about. This was surprising and disappointing, for her profile was in most respects similar to that of *Wanderer III*, who lay a-hull so well. I concluded that her desire to bear away might be due to the steering defect which, with the wind as it was on the port side, would be trying to turn her away from it. Alternatively it might have been due to the windage of the rolled-up jib, or to the mast having been moved by the designer six inches forward of where he had placed it on the original sail plan. It could have been a combination of all three.

However, she shipped only one heavy crest into the cockpit, and some of this got below by way of the hinged cockpit seat which the builders had optimistically thought to be watertight. Immediately after the crest had burst aboard I was alerted by the unusual noise of water rushing about in the bilge, which until then had been dry; so I manned the Whale Gusher pump, which was conveniently situated in the oilskin locker by the companionway and could be worked from a sitting or standing position, and pumped out about 10 gallons. I had taken such quick action because the bilge was shallow and rather flat, and if water were allowed to accumulate there it could, with such wild motion, get sluiced up into some of the lockers. Incidentally, with the importance of a dry bilge in mind, I had obtained from Munster Simms, makers of the Whale pumps, one of their special strumboxes in which a valve was fitted to prevent any water remaining in pump or hose from running back into the bilge. Susan made us cups of hot cocoa, we turned in and surprisingly slept quite well for a few hours after we had warmed up.

By noon the wind had dropped to 25 knots and in the afternoon we managed to seize new slugs to the luff of the sail, but as the sea, which was of no great height, was still rough and we needed more rest, we left the ship lying under bare poles until dawn, then made sail and headed once more towards our destination, making an allowance for the East Australian Current which could be expected to sweep strongly to the south along the coast.

In the evening we made a landfall, as intended, on the North Solitary Islands, 30 miles north of Coffs Harbour, spent the night jilling about between them and South Solitary, motoring from time to time in the failing wind to stem the current, and entered Coffs Harbour, which we had not wanted to do in the dark, before breakfast. The water police came out in their launch to meet us – among other things they perform much the same service as is carried out by the R.N.L.I. at home; indeed, the very next day they plucked two men from a broken-down runabout close to the beach in an onshore gale – and asked us to anchor in the outer harbour until doctor and customs had been on board. As the day was a public holiday it was not possible to get a berth allotted to us in the marina, so as another gale was expected to arrive in the night the police led us into the inner harbour to berth at their own little jetty in a very snug corner, took our lines and rigged up a hose so that we could wash off the salt with which everything was caked. They and everyone else we met were so kind and helpful that we felt we had arrived among friends.

*   *   *

After a couple of days at the police jetty we moved to the marina which had only recently been completed. Although we usually preferred the privacy and independence of lying at anchor, stopping at a marina for a short time was always a pleasant change. There was something rather cozy about that one, and of course it was convenient: the ability to step ashore at any time without having to make a trip by dinghy, to stand and dream and admire our ship close to at leisure, to take the half hour walk along the harbour wall, over the sandy, windswept flats and across the railway tracks, where in the early morning I was able to watch the north-bound sleeper with its two locomotives rumbling through, and on into the little town of Coffs Harbour Jetty to do the shopping; but our chief entertainment was meeting the other live-aboards.

Notable among these was Jeané Rouse-Upjohn, M.A., J.P., who lived with her Denis aboard the converted R.A.A.F. rescue launch *Ranji*. She ran a small business which found jobs for those who needed them, or people to do jobs for those who could not do them for themselves; in addition she was a journalist, and it was in that capacity that she made herself known to us, for she wished to write a story for the local paper about *Wanderer V*. Even above the noise of seas breaking against the harbour walls her voice carried clearly across the water, for it was of the kind that 'shatters glass', yet Jeané was a gentle, kindly lady. She did all manner of things to help make our stay enjoyable and interesting, driving us about to see something of the countryside, which had splendid forests, and many banana plantations among which stood Big Banana, a tourist trap, where she treated us to chocolate-coated bananas out of a freezer—not easy eating in mid-afternoon. She also took us to the Plaza, an out-of-town shopping complex, where in one department under strip-lights that receded into the far distance lay acres of women's clothing, rack upon rack of dresses, skirts and shirts, slacks and shorts and underwear in overwhelming profusion. The owner of the local shipyard, where the previous night vandals had set fire to and destroyed the fibreglass mould in which he had planned to build one fishing vessel a year, and his wife took us to dine at one of the row of little restaurants that lined one side of the main street; there to our surprise and embarrassment (though not, I think, to hers) we found Jeané serving as a waitress and doing the washing-up. Denis came in later and dined alone.

While at the marina we got to know the English couple Tim and Pauline Carr, who had sailed their lovely old Falmouth quay punt *Curlew* out from Europe and had lived aboard her for many years. With her plumb ends, long bowsprit, gaff rig and tan sails *Curlew* was an attraction wherever she went and had made a great reputation for herself in local racing events. The Carrs took their racing seriously and had lightened the old cutter as much as they could; they had recently removed the watertanks, for as Pauline pointed out, 'Even empty tanks weigh something.' While discussing our steering problem with them I had said that we would need not only a good slip to haul out on – the one at Coffs Harbour would have done very well – but some expert professional advice. The Carrs suggested that we contact Joe Adams, one of Australia's leading yacht designers who had befriended them when they were in the Sydney area. We decided to sail south and consult him.

The coast of New South Wales, which comprises mile upon mile of golden beaches broken by occasional bold headlands and shallow river mouths backed by distant mountains, extends in a north/south direction for about 550 miles, Coffs Harbour lying near its northern boundary with Queensland. In my view it is singularly lacking in good harbours, though the Australians who cruise so enthusiastically there would be unlikely to agree with me. Apart from Coffs, the only harbours which appeared to be safe to enter or leave in any weather or sea conditions were Port Stephens, Broken Bay and Port Jackson (Sydney). The rest were in rivers, and very fine some of them were, but although the building of breakwaters and training walls had improved many of the entrances, all had bars on which in some circumstances the sea could heap up dangerously or break. We nearly lost *Wanderer III* and ourselves in one of those bars—that of the Richmond River which is generally considered to be one of the best—and had no wish to attempt to cross one again.

We therefore sailed direct for Port Stephens, and had an uneventful overnight trip. We did not get any help from the south-setting current, which is reported to have a speed of from four to five knots, for it was not running then. This was in marked contrast to its performance on our last trip when we were trying to get north and spent 18 hours beating against wind and current off Tacking Point—so aptly named by Cook who had the same problem there—and at the end of that period found we had lost four miles.

Over the years Port Stephens had changed; there were scores of yachts in every sheltered corner, marinas and oyster farms had grown up, and where before we had walked a sandy track to buy stores at the village of Nelson's Bay, now was a traffic-torn highway and a rash of new houses, jostling one another for a glimpse of the water, and the village had become a holiday town. However, the wide harbour was still attractive and offered several excellent anchorages.

Since the distance between Port Stephens and Broken Bay was only 80 miles and we did not wish to arrive in the dark because of the likely profusion of dazzling lights ashore which in most built-up areas make pilotage by night so difficult, we were not at all concerned when the wind fell light as we left Port Stephens, for we had most of the day and all of the night before us. There was no sea and very little swell, the day was sunny but not unpleasantly hot as we sailed slowly south. Being becalmed at suppertime we ate the meal together in a civilised manner at the saloon table, and agreed that afterwards we would motor on a bit. We were doing the washing up when a southerly buster sprang upon us without warning: there had been no drop of the barograph, no roll of cloud, and we had failed to listen to weather forecasts which usually predicted those southerly wind changes and their expected times of arrival with a fair degree of accuracy. The jib had already been rolled up to stop it chafing on the shrouds in the calm, and so sudden and strong was the wind that we did not bother with the first reef in the mainsail but pulled down the second one straightaway, a slovenly action, but as has already been seen reefing took us a long time. Then we set up the inner forestay and bent on and set the staysail. The fine day had lulled us into a state of complacency and the arrival of wind had caught us unprepared: the boathook was not lashed, windlass cover not on, naval pipe unplugged, turnbuttons on locker doors not secured and sheets tangled in the cockpit.

By the time we had the ship snugged down and everything in order night was upon us and the sky, which had been pale blue all day, was now covered with black cloud on the low-slung underbelly of which the lights of industrial Newcastle, extending both ways as far as one could see, glowed with a sinister aspect. The sea grew short and rough, as one might expect it to when a 35-knot wind blows against a current, and seemed to have arisen with the same speed as the wind. Driving rain stung our faces when we peered over the hood to look for shipping. It was indeed a wretched night and for the first time in many years I felt sick. We could not lay along the land and twice had to make offshore tacks in the neighbourhood of Norah Head, where there are shoal patches on which the sea is reported to break.

After several hours the wind moderated a little and we could have done with a bit more of the mainsail, but as I have said we had taken in only the second reef and to shake that out and then tuck in the first reef was more than we felt prepared to do in so short and steep a sea. How easy it would have been had we had roller gear.

So we plunged slowly on for the rest of the night, and began to realise that it was no longer a matter of not wanting to reach Broken Bay before daylight; the question now was would we ever get there before the following night? However, the wind took off some more, the sea became less steep, we got some more sail set, and with a little help from the engine entered Broken Bay around noon.

The name is misleading, for that place is not a bay in the accepted sense of the term, but is a remarkable area of land-locked water with one river, the Hawkesbury, flowing into it and several crooked arms thrusting into hilly country, one of them at least 10 miles in length (chart C). There are no shoals, no rock dangers, very little tidal stream and, as all the land was a national park of almost untouched bush and forest, there were few roads and hardly any houses. The one exception to this was Pittwater, the arm that runs south for five miles immediately within the entrance. The head of this was 20 miles from the centre of Sydney, and suburbs extended all the way to crowd most of the arm's eastern shore, terminating abruptly where the sandy isthmus runs on a mile to Barranjoey with its lighthouse. For the Sydney yachtsman, Pittwater—though physically it bears no resemblance—is his Hamble River, packed with thousands of sailing and power yachts; even from the entrance we could see the thickets of masts though the craft were hull-down, and feeling in no fit state after our rough night at sea to go looking for a berth in that crowded place, we continued up the western arm and anchored in the smooth, green water and perfect shelter of Refuge Bay, a place in which we had sought sanctuary in the past. After a silent night and a glorious dawn chorus we retraced our steps and made our way up Pittwater to seek a berth and Joe Adams.

The difficulty for the stranger is to find a space among the mass of moorings in which to anchor, and yet be within reasonable dinghy reach of a landing place, but we thought that the Royal Prince Alfred Yacht Club, which lay near the head of Pittwater and within walking distance of the shops at Newport, might help us. The club was known to us, for on our last visit we had given a talk and slide show there and had been rewarded with a fine cooked ham, which came in useful on the way back to our ship when we met a starving kitten and were able to feed it on a hunk hacked out of that splendid piece of meat.

The big-hearted club at once took us in. The dockmaster showed us to a berth in the 300-berth marina; the manager/ secretary said we were not to pay anything and made us honorary members for a month, so we had the run of the place. It was a fine club with a friendly, willing staff, several quick, clean and efficient hauling-out arrangements with plenty of hard standing, a dining room and two bars, in one of which we bought the club's own blend of scotch labelled 'The Alfreds',

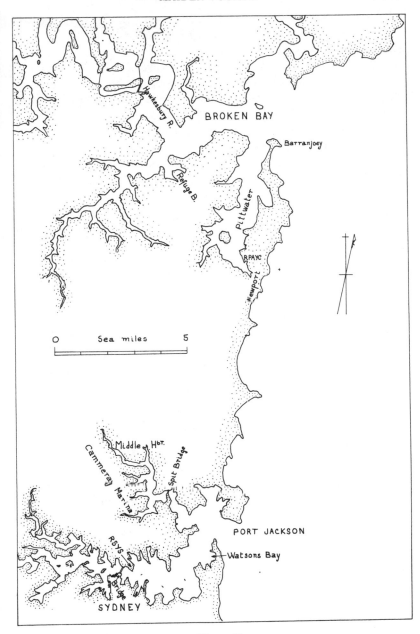

Chart C

enormous changing rooms—I had a choice of eighteen shower stalls in mine—and in the grounds a well-stocked chandlery which gave us a generous discount on the many things we bought there. Perhaps the most remarkable thing about the Alfred in these days, when so many clubs have difficulty in making both ends meet, was that it was not only alive and solvent but actually made a profit.

Although the activities of the club mostly revolved round racing, several members were most kind and generous to us. One presented us with a strobe light for our lifebuoy, a thing we had been unable to obtain at any chandlers. Another, who had owned 13 sailing and 5 power yachts, asked us aboard for drinks, and when we left we were the richer by two bottles of good Australian wine, an up-to-date chart of Broken Bay on which he had marked his favourite anchorages, and a big helping of prawns for our supper. In the morning he brought us everything we might want for breakfast, and said he hoped this would atone for the harder side of some Australians; but he need not have been concerned on that score, for on this, our fourth visit to his country, we had been treated with every consideration.

One of the first things we did was telephone Joe Adams. That brilliant man had designed some of the fastest yachts in the country yet—perhaps because he had made a circumnavigation with his wife—he well understood the need for simplicity and seaworthiness in a short-handed cruising yacht. He came for a sail next day to judge the steering defect for himself, then took us to his nearby office and, by telephone, started to organise some of our other requirements, such as stainless steel slugs for the mainsail, and a new and lighter boom fitted with roller reefing gear; the latter took more doing than one might have expected. At first the sparmaker said no round extrusion suitable for us (6 in diameter) was available and we would have to make do with an oval one; this of course we declined, but when Joe pointed out that we were quite prepared to have a wood boom and that he had a shipwright ready lined up to make it, a round alloy spar soon appeared. Gibb and Lewmar in England were contacted by telex, but neither could provide a reefing gear—we wondered where other people got theirs—and eventually an Australian-made gear was procured.

Meanwhile the club hauled us out and Joe, together with Hank Kauffman, a retired shipwright friend of his who had taken up the breeding of racing horses, were standing by before we were fully out of the water. They quickly saw what was wrong, and pointed it out to us as we climbed down the ladder. The alterations made in New Zealand—lengthened keel, more nearly upright sternpost, and new rudder—had not been properly faired; the rudder had more round on its port than on its starboard side and the deadwood was slightly more concave on the starboard than on the port side. Joe was convinced that this asymmetry had been acting like a trim-tab, causing the bias to starboard.

While Susan and I scrubbed the bottom, Hank went off to take a mare to stud, then collected tools and materials and within two days had faired the defects and coated them with dynel and epoxy, and after we had applied a coat of anti-fouling paint we were launched with him and Joe on board.

As we moved out from the cradle under power we found that *Wanderer* now had a tendency to turn to port, as indeed she should with her right-handed propeller, but the most rewarding moment came when we started to sail. No longer did she demand a heavy hand on the tiller to keep her on course; only a couple of fingers on the helm were needed in a moderate breeze, and with the mainsheet eased a trifle she steered herself on the wind unattended. Of course we were absolutely delighted and so, I believe, were Joe and Hank who seemed also to be impressed with the yacht's speed. By chance we met the Carrs in *Curlew* sailing in, and they turned to pace us. A slippery looking yacht was passing under power, and she must have had a brush with the English yacht for someone aboard her shouted across to us, 'You won't catch that one.' But much to our astonishment we did and even overtook her when the wind freshened a bit; but when it fell light *Curlew*, with her big topsail (and no watertanks), was the faster. That memorable day we discovered that our awkward, hard-helmed fidgety bitch had changed her manners to those of a gentle lady, and from that time on we enjoyed day sailing in those pleasantly smooth though overcrowded waters in a vessel that was now fun to handle. It must, however, be said that when well heeled in a strong wind she still carried a lot of weather helm, and with her broad quarters no doubt she always would, but was still quite manageable.

After some delay the new boom arrived. It looked too long, and was by 12 inches, so back it had to go to the factory. After its return when we rolled down an experimental reef we saw that because the reefing gear had been designed in the days when every mainsail had a thick hemp boltrope on its luff, it possessed a narrow neck to accommodate this; but like most modern mainsails ours had a very small boltrope and, when rolled down, a great strain came on the cloth in way of the first slide along the foot. As a temporary measure I overcame this by building up the neck with a rope serving and wood batten, but a few days later Joe arrived with a split alloy sleeve and made a neat and proper job of it. That was the last of his many kindnesses, and it was with sadness that we said goodbye to that helpful and generous man and put to sea to try out our new toys, which now included a 100-square foot trysail. We had that sail made as a standby in case the mainsail ever got damaged and we hoped that under it alone *Wanderer* would heave-to properly in heavy weather and thus avoid the need to lie a-hull, which she had shown she was not very good at doing.

We stood offshore for about 30 miles, then headed south, keeping parallel to the coast. On two successive days gale warnings were broadcast, so we bent on the new sail. This involved removing all the mainsail slugs from the mast-groove and inserting the trysail slugs; this would not have been easy to do in a gale, and the sailmaker had made it even more difficult by fitting such long slugs that when they were stacked in the groove it was not possible, from on deck, to reach the head of the sail and shackle on the halyard, so we replaced every other slug with a shorter one. We realised that to enable the sail to be bent on and set with some degree of convenience we would need to have a proper track fitted to the mast for the mainsail and another alongside it for the trysail, but as that would entail unstepping the mast it would have to wait until we returned to New Zealand. As the forecast gale came to nothing we never did discover if the trysail was effective or not, and turning round we made our way north to Port Jackson.

Our time in Australia coincided with 'the great dry', the worst drought the country had ever experienced; in parts of New South Wales there had been no worthwhile rain for four years. Lack of grass had caused the death of countless sheep and cattle, others had been shot by farmers to save them from starvation, and high winds picked up the powder-dry topsoil and carried it away out to sea in huge dust clouds. During our abortive trysail test that sail, together with the rest of the ship and her gear, became coated with dust; all her white running rigging turned brown and was to remain so for some months— we had known nothing like it since we were in a sand storm in the Gulf of Suez.

At the time of the drought enormous bush fires raged through the tinder-dry forests, consuming everything in their paths and, in Victoria and South Australia, left in their wakes 70 people dead and 8,000 homeless. It was therefore not only with dust that we were covered, but also with ash from those great fires.

The latitude of Sydney is about 34°S, yet in that neighbourhood we experienced temperatures almost as high as we had known in any other part of the world. In Broken Bay on several afternoons the cabin thermometer rose to 108°F (42°C) and under the brassy sun and smoky sky the hard wind beat hot and dry on one's body as though coming from some giant oven.

Our admiration for the Australians who take such a harsh climate in their stride rose even higher during this visit, and oh how we longed for there to be some rain to extinguish the infernos and bring the parched country back to life. I quote Dorothea Mackellar:

> Core of my heart, my country!
> Her pitiless blue sky,
> When sick at heart around us
> We see the cattle die—
> But then the grey clouds gather,
> And we can hear again
> The drumming of an army,
> The steady, soaking rain.

*　　　*　　　*

Sailing into the heart of a great city is always rewarding and exciting. Port Jackson was full of life, bustle and colour that day, and traffic thickened as the Sydney opera house and harbour bridge came into view. So vast are those erections that we got the scale wrong, and when Circular Quay began to open up from behind the opera house and the stern of a white ship appeared, it looked so small that for a little while we did not realise it belonged to *Canberra*, lately returned to the tourist trade after the Falklands war. A bulk carrier outward bound was dwarfed by the bridge as she crept under it, and as we came into the broad shadow of the bridge the roar and rumble of rail and road traffic overhead fell upon us. There we seemed to be trapped in a web of creaming criss-crossed wakes left by swift hydrofoils, lumbering ferries, and speeding launches belonging to navy, customs and harbourboard. In Port Jackson all commercial vessels have right of way over pleasure craft, and on one occasion it looked as though we would never avoid a collision with one of the ferries, no matter how we twisted and turned, for she seemed determined to get closer and closer, and when she was almost alongside her wheelhouse door opened, a head poked out and a voice said: 'Hullo Hiscocks! How long are you staying in Sinny?' A yachtie we presumed.

Above the bridge we looked in at Lavender Bay, thinking we might anchor there. But Luna Park, a gigantic fun-fair, sprawled right beside it, and the amplified music from many sources, the clatter of the coasters topped by the screams of their terrified passengers, and the shrieks of children in the swimming pool combined to make such a cacophony that we decided against it. We therefore retreated back beneath the bridge, beat down to near the harbour mouth, turned towards Middle Harbour and waited in the queue for the Spit Bridge to open and let us in. As it did so a ferry jumped the queue and went ahead fast; her wash caught us and made us roll heavily just as we were passing the bridge and for an awful moment it looked as though our mast was going to foul its uplifted bascule.

After the excitements of that busy day it was good to secure to a swinging mooring in a narrow arm of Middle Harbour off

Cammeray Marina. That welcoming little place was surely unique in two respects: it was inhabited by a gaggle of geese acting as bodyguard to a handsome black swan, and its only access to the shore was by way of a steep flight of 106 steps; at one time it had a miniature cog railway to bring down stores and equipment, but that had been wrecked by local children who could not be prevented from playing with it.

Although the almost vertical marina side of the creek was tightly packed with tier upon tier of houses, the other shore was native bush, a haven for birds. There were waders, cockatoos, kingfishers and blue herons, and last thing at night and first thing in the morning the place reverberated with the raucous and infectious laughter of a pair of kookaburras.

In another arm of Middle Harbour we found a silent anchorage away from buildings and roads, and taking the dinghy we rowed to its head, in among a wilderness of mangroves and on until the creek was restricted by precipitous rock walls. It seemed remarkable that such an attractive oasis could exist within two miles of the roaring harbour bridge, under which we had so recently sailed.

Throughout our time in N.S.W. the weather pattern remained almost constant. Usually the nights were calm, but in the forenoon a breeze made from north-east or south-east and by mid-afternoon had reached a speed of 20 to 30 knots, sometimes more, only to drop away after nightfall. This pattern was disturbed at intervals of a few days, or sometimes weeks, by the wind blowing from north-west and followed by a southerly wind change such as we had experienced while at sea off Newcastle.

Many voyaging people plan their ocean passages on information obtained from the U.S. pilot charts. For the South Pacific these are published one for each quarter, and the chart for December/February had something very odd about it likely to disturb anyone planning to sail through the 5° square in which Sydney is situated, and the next square to the east, as we were soon to do, for the Beaufort scale force of the winds, indicated by the number of feathers on each directional arrow, showed extremely violent weather. In the first square the south and south-east arrows were given an *average* of Force 8, and in the other square the feathers showed that winds from south-west and south-east averaged Force 9, and the south arrow had ten feathers on it—even Cape Horn, which appeared on the same chart, was not credited with such strong winds—yet in the small inset chart giving the percentages of gales for the quarter, no gales were shown in the first square and only three gales in the second. One might suppose that some draughtsman in the U.S. weather bureau had been feather happy the day he drew those arrows, but he could shake one's confidence in the accuracy of the rest of that chart, or indeed in other charts in the series.

Of course pilot charts do not purport to forecast the weather, they merely tell us what the average weather has been over many years based on observations made by seamen, and I found I had to remind myself about that word 'average'. For example, on the chart to which I have just referred the North Island of New Zealand appears to have almost perfect sailing weather: no wind arrows have more than four feathers, and none have less than three. However, having spent much time sailing in that area, I discovered that those apparently pleasant conditions were made up as follows: for five days there was not enough wind to fill a light-weather sail, and on the sixth and seventh days the wind blew with gale force. A strange thing was that calm periods or gales in those waters occurred just as often with a high barometer as with a low one—no wonder weather forecasting is such a chancy business.

For our final few days in Port Jackson the Royal Sydney Yacht Squadron kindly provided us with a mooring and gave us the run of its delightful rabbit-warren of a club house at Kirribilli on the northern shore. From there we went to Sydney by ferry and discovered what a gracious way that is for commuters to get to work. How much better it must be to stroll down the hill from home to ferry pier and travel smoothly and silently across the harbour into the city, than to go frustratedly there by road in the rush hour.

Last time we had been in Sydney it was in an uproar with pneumatic drills and earth-moving machines, for the underground railway was being built. Now all that was finished, and as we strolled along the broad sidewalks, which were coolly shaded from the sun by the high-rise buildings, we were much impressed. The city had a certain grace and charm, as indeed had many of its people; the girls, in particular, were bronzed and well turned out, and they looked proud of themselves as they strode along with heads held high and breasts out-thrust.

At the immigration office we were handed papers to fill in at our leisure, and made a date for the customs launch to meet us in Watsons Bay near the harbour entrance, for the rule was that outward-bound yachts must anchor there on the day of departure for the paper work to be completed. We were a bit concerned about this for, while going alongside *Stella Ilimo*, the little sloop belonging to Ann Gash and in which she, the 'voyaging grandmother from Australia', had circumnavigated single-handed, the customs launch damaged the yacht so badly that she was delayed for several weeks. However, the coxswain who brought the customs officer off to us handled his launch so well that she did not even touch us, and he lay off while the paperwork was being done.

*   *   *

In preparation for what was to be our fourth crossing of the Tasman Sea – that notorious south-west corner of the mighty Pacific – I had fabricated and fitted a number of stout, brass turnbuttons to ensure that when we were flung on to our beam-ends or 'capsized', as is now so fashionable, the contents of bilges and lockers would remain in place. I had even managed to secure the potentially lethal lid of the ice-box without defiling its formica top. With the possibility of strong headwinds we did not wish to overload the ship, so we left one of the three watertanks empty and did not top up with fuel. We need not have taken those precautions, however, and the shortage of fuel proved to be something of a handicap, for during the 1,200-mile passage we had some calms and not often did the wind exceed 10 knots. For the first few days it was dead ahead, so that neither tack was the more favourable, but after that it was mostly abaft the beam or right aft.

Unless one is prepared to use the auxiliary engine, there is obviously only one way of getting a sailing vessel to move along in a light breeze and that is to set a large sail (or sails) made of very light material. For this purpose spinnakers of one form or another have been used for a long time, but a spinnaker needs a boom and calls for special care in handling and steering and a large enough crew for the purpose; even then it may wrap itself around the forestay or crosstrees, or get up to some other mischief. Nevertheless some single-handers, even light-weight ones such as Clare Francis, appear to have managed with a fair degree of success, but Susan and I believed that if we were to use a spinnaker we would get ourselves into real trouble sooner or later.

Well aware of the mistrust that most short-handed cruising people have of the spinnaker, sailmakers have devised a light-weather sail which they claim will work with the apparent wind from forward of the beam to right aft *without the need for a pole or boom*. Most of them have dreamed up special names for such sails: Cruising Chute, Multi-purpose Sail, Gennaker, Loafer, Easy Rider, Lazybones, etc. Each claims that his product has the above remarkable qualities and I thought how wonderful it would be if this was true, for then with such a sail to help us along our passages would be much faster and more fun. Of course the sensible way of finding out would have been to borrow one of suitable size and try it; but I was too impatient, and perhaps too easily persuaded by clever advertising, and decided that we should make *Wanderer* a present of such a sail immediately her steering defect had been cured. I therefore got in touch with a Sydney firm of sailmakers, and an enormous scarlet and white affair, which they told us measured 818 square feet, soon arrived.

Such a sail, which is set flying (i.e. not hanked to a stay), usually has a luff equal in length to that of the topmast stay, and is much longer on the foot than is a spinnaker, perhaps $1\frac{1}{2}$ times the base of the fore-triangle, and its clew is higher than its tack—in other words it is an oversize, unhanked, light genoa. It is said that the sail is just the thing for a cruising man and his wife as it is so easy to get in the lee of the mainsail, and to take it in one just lets fly the tack and pulls the sail into the cockpit, again in the lee of the mainsail, as the halyard is eased away. But this part of the business seemed to me to call for at least three people: one to steer, one to let go the halyard and another to drag in the huge bag of nylon; with only the two of us on board I could see problems arising in a suddenly freshening wind, especially at night. In spite of their claims, some of the sailmakers appear to agree with me for they have made available certain devices to simplify setting and handing and, like the sails themselves, these have been given a variety of names: Snuffer, Squeezer, Scoop, Sock, etc.

We had ours fitted with a Squeezer. This consists of a nylon sausage-skin with a metal hoop at its lower end into which the sail is stuffed. The upper end of the skin is secured to the head of the sail, and there is a small block there. A line made fast to the hoop passes up inside the skin among the folds of the sail, through the block, then down outside the skin–where it passes through a few brass rings to control it–through the tack cringle and then back to the hoop. The sail is hoisted in sausage form and its tack is made fast at the stemhead; the sheet is led outside the rigging to a fairlead or block on the quarter and thence to a sheet winch. All is now ready for setting. The foredeck hand hauls on the line to pull the hoop, and with it the nylon skin, up to the masthead; the sail in all its colourful glory blossoms and the helmsman sheets it in. To furl the sail the sheet is let go, the foredeck hand hauls on the other part of the line to pull down the hoop and skin, thus gathering the sail and stuffing it back into sausage form.

We played with our new sail in the smooth water of Broken Bay and found it almost impossible to entice the clew out of the hoop because the clew patch was so large and stiff, the makers apparently having the idea that we would be carrying the sail in 20 knots or more of wind instead of under 10 knots, which we regarded as being the limit for our strength. Presumably for the same reason, they made the sail of material that I believe was unnecessarily heavy. Had the clew been within comfortable reach I could have juggled it out of the hoop, but I could barely reach it while standing on tiptoe at the forward end of the cabin top, and that was something I did not intend to do at sea. Susan therefore took a tuck in the sock with the idea that the clew would then not be able to enter and get stuck, but this left too much of the sail on the loose. Therefore the sail had to go back to its makers for alterations to clew and sock, not once but twice.

Because the bagged sail was so bulky and heavy it was difficult to stow in the forepeak, so I lazily took to leaving it on the sole of the sleeping cabin, where of course it got moved about and trampled on, with the result that when we came to use it we found the sail twisted in its skin and its line tangled. So the sail had to be taken down and repacked with its luff and leech parallel and the line neatly in between them. To do this on deck was impossible if there was any wind at all, so we had to stretch out sail and sock below, and since its length exceeded the yacht's overall length, it was a frustrating and time-consuming operation which we had to repeat on several occasions.

Out in the Tasman we quickly discovered that it is one thing to use this kind of sail in smooth water but quite another to do so at sea. The only way that I could masthead the slippery sausage single-handed was to hoist it straight out through the forehatch, but the motion, even in the very slight swell running that day, was enough to cause the sausage to swing out and aft so that before I could get it fully up it had got round the lee crosstree, from which it was not easily disentangled.

However, we got the sail set eventually and took up our course for the northern tip of New Zealand; this brought the wind well abaft the beam and at once the dawdling ship picked up her skirts and moved; but then she rolled, not much of a roll but enough to put the sail momentarily in the lee of the mainsail and it collapsed, quite dead; then *Wanderer* rolled the other way and the sail filled with an almighty crash. This happened repeatedly and we wondered if the rigging could stand it for long, certainly we could not. So we altered course to bring the wind more on the beam, but even that did not keep the sail quiet, so we took it in, boomed out the staysail and proceeded slowly but peacefully on our way.

It may be wondered perhaps why we did not boom out the big sail like a spinnaker, but because of the great length of its foot compared with that of a conventional spinnaker, the sail requires a very long boom if it is not to become unstable and perhaps wrap itself up round the forestay, and as our forestay already had 400 square feet of jib rolled up on it we were not prepared to take the risk. I conclude from our brief trials with it that the multi-purpose sail is not of much value in an ocean-going yacht except when the wind is on the beam and with us that condition has been so rare that in spite of the generous discount given us by the sailmakers, we reckon our sail has cost us about £100 a mile.

It is clear that I am no authority, but I make the following observations in the hope that they may be of interest to anyone thinking of investing in one of these sails.

Since the pull at the masthead is not forward as it is with a hanked-on sail, but is athwartships, one should not use it with a conventional halyard passing over a sheave at the masthead as that might cause damage to the sheave box and is almost certain to chafe the halyard. A spinnaker halyard, i.e. one led through a block outside the topmost stay, should be used and it should be attached to the head of the sail via a swivel, so that any twists in sausage or sail will straighten themselves out. The strains imposed even in a light breeze are considerable and since the tack as well as the halyard needs to be eased off as the wind comes farther aft, the tack line should be handled by a winch of sufficient power, otherwise it will not be possible to get it in again, and it has to be got in before one can reach the furling line which passes through the tack cringle. If it is intended that the sail, when running, is to be boomed out like a spinnaker, it will probably be more satisfactory to go in for a proper spinnaker in the first place because of the excessively long boom the other sail demands, but of course it was in an attempt to dispense with a boom that this sail was invented. Finally, it might be no bad thing if sailmakers would add a rider to their evocative advertisements extolling the virtues of this type of sail; it should read IN SMOOTH WATER, then people as gullible as I am might not so easily be misled.

As well as the clemency of the weather, a notable feature throughout the 12-day passage was the succession of very heavy dews; every evening soon after sunset, deck and sails were running with water just as though there had been rain. Twice we were visited and escorted for half an hour or so by a party of completely black creatures whistling so loudly that we could clearly hear them on deck. At first and at a little distance we took them to be porpoises, for their wheeling/breathing actions were porpoise-like, though unusually ponderous; but as they gathered close around us and we realised their great length and girth, we reckoned they must be whales, but which sort? Our book on sea-mammals was of no help, for it explained that the only sure way of distinguishing one kind of whale from another is to count the number of vertebrae.

A thunderstorm with fresh squalls met us near North Cape, and when it had flickered and rumbled away there was glassy calm and not even any swell after we had rounded the headland and put the Tasman astern; so we used our small remaining stock of fuel to motor to our home port and arrived there only just in time, for that same afternoon the wind set in from the east and blew hard without a let-up for the next ten days.

*   *   *

It is difficult to compare the individuals in our line of *Wanderer*s because their vital statistics varied so widely and the line spanned some fifty years, during which our opinions and criteria tended to change as we gained more seagoing experience.

Wanderer I was a very old 18-footer with plumb ends and a long, straight keel. I do not believe she had many merits, and she never made an offshore passage, but I did learn the rudiments of sailing in her. *Wanderer II* was a simple but characterful 23-foot gaff cutter designed for me by Jack Laurent Giles and in most respects was similar to his famous Vertue Class. Sailing her single-handed in British and French waters I discovered the joys and sorrows of gaff rig: the ability to set a large area of working sail and reduce it quickly by taking in the topsail, but the rigging was complex and prone to chafe and windward ability was impaired as soon as the big topsail had been handed. After Susan and I had sailed her from Falmouth to the Azores and back we concluded she was a bit too small for ocean voyaging, for which that trip had given us an appetite, and sold her to Bill Howell who, with a companion, immediately sailed her out to Tahiti (showing how wrong we had been) and then took her on single-handed to Hawaii. *Wanderer III* was also from the drawing board of Jack Giles, a 30-foot sloop with a

beam of 8½ feet, a draught of 5½ feet and a 4-h.p. engine—our
first ever. She took us competently around the world twice and
our only reason for selling her was that we wished to live
permanently afloat and considered she was too small to carry
the many possessions we believed we ought to have in a floating
home. So *Wanderer IV* was built, the 49-foot steel ketch designed
by Van der Meer and featured in Part I of this book. Among
other voyages, she took us round the world and half way round
again. I have already given our reasons for selling her.

Because of her size, *IV* was much more comfortable at sea
than any of the others, and could keep going in a freshening
wind from forward of the beam longer than they could have
done. Whether she was the most seaworthy I cannot say;
certainly she came through some violent weather without any
trouble (hove-to, a-hull, or running), notably off the Cape and
in the Tasman Sea; but so, in other waters, did *III*, though her
motion was of course much more tiring. Perhaps because we
owned her longer than any of the others and she carried us
further, we had more affection for her, though we were well
aware of her shortcomings. Among these was her narrow beam
which cramped the accommodation and, I believe, may have
been the cause of her fast and furious rolling, in that to keep
upright she depended too much on her ballast keel and lacked
initial stability. She was small enough and handy enough to
wriggle in or out of small or crowded places and maintaining
her was easy, particularly her underwater body which, being
copper-sheathed, needed no paint until, in time, the copper
became oxidised. Fortunately she was easy to steer, for her first
two long voyages were made in the days before wind vane
steering gears had been perfected.

How *Wanderer V* compares with her predecessors has in some
respects yet to be ascertained, although she has made good
some 6,700 sea miles since her launching. We have now been
living aboard continuously for eighteen months, and in port
find her almost as comfortable and convenient as big *IV*,
though the restless way she sheers about when at anchor and
the condensation in cold weather, due to lack of insulation, is
tiresome. So far maintenance has been just as easy and enjoyable as it was with *II* and *III*, and I see no reason for it to

increase. In smooth water she is more fun to sail than were any of the others, no doubt because she is faster and more easily driven and, compared with gaff cutter *II* and ketch *IV* is close-winded, but when well heeled her heavy weather helm is disconcerting, particularly in squally weather. She has not met a gale at sea since the steering metamorphosis, so we do not know if she will now lie quietly when hove-to, or if she will respond to the vane gear under all conditions, nor do we know if she will run surely and steadily before a big following sea, for although she certainly ran before more than one gale after leaving New Zealand on her maiden voyage, the sea was then of no great height or steepness. If she shows she can do these things I believe that as an all-round cruiser/voyager she should serve us very well.

PART IV
The Changed Scene

The changes which have come about in the design, construction and equipment of yachts are obvious to anyone who has been involved with boats over the past 10 to 15 years, but for one like myself, who has witnessed the scene for some 50 years, the revolution is quite remarkable.

In the U.K. in the early 1930s cruising was the pleasure of the fortunate few; each yacht differed from all others, each had a character of her own, each could be recognised by 'the cut of her jib', and with but few exceptions each was built of wood. Sails were of cotton or flax, heavy when wet and subject to attack by mildew unless aired frequently; standing rigging was of galvanised steel or iron, and running rigging of hemp or manilla, which needed much attention because it shrank when wet and stretched when dry. Many of the smaller yachts had no auxiliary engines, and to give steerage way in a calm most carried a long sweep for sculling over the stern, so it was important to work the winds and tides to advantage. People who did possess engines – they ran on petrol or paraffin, and the former were often two-stroke – could not always rely on them starting when needed, so manoeuvring was largely done under sail, and as electricity was little used cabin and navigation lamps burnt paraffin. There was no refrigeration, and in the U.K. no ice-boxes. Radio, if available, comprised a simple receiving set powered by an 'accumulator' and a 'high tension' battery of 110 volts. As boatyards were few and far between, and the hoist or travel-lift had not been invented, bottoms were scrubbed and anti-fouled between tides, either standing on a hard with legs rigged out, or alongside a quay or wall. For coastwise navigation one used a compass, a Walker's log, a chart, a pair of dividers and parallel rules, and a leadline; on an offshore passage a sextant, chronometer and books of tables were added. In foul weather one wore stiff oilskins and sou'wester or a Breton fisherman's smock, and they did not keep the wet out for very long.

Creeks, rivers and estuaries offered clean, uncrowded anchorages for the visitor. Most members of the cruising fraternity knew one another, or quickly came to do so because of the camaraderie which was a delightful feature of those simple, faraway days which had much in common with the early days of the motor car. I look back on them with affection and nostalgia, but I do not believe I would want to live and cruise in them again.

Today the design of the cruising/voyaging yacht has in many respects followed that of the racing yacht, with light displacement requiring a comparatively small sail area, fin keel and separate rudder to reduce wetted surface, and a high-aspect rig which is efficient to windward—all resulting in a fast and weatherly vessel. With efficiency, speed, and ease of mass-production to the fore, much of the old grace and charm has left the scene. Sheer has almost vanished along with the counter stern; sterns are commonly retrorse now, thus reducing deck area and stowage space aft where the cruiser might be glad of it. Freeboard has increased to provide headroom in the shallow hull, and attempts to disguise it are commonly made with exotic paint schemes or strips of colour tape. Chain cables and anchors of adequate size are frowned on because of their weight; compact and efficient engines capable of driving modern yachts as fast as they can normally go under sail, i.e. at hull speed, are commonly installed and, because of their thin and well-engineered construction in grp, these yachts have more space below deck than older ones of similar length. There is now a certain sterile uniformity about the fleets with their tall, white rigs which are so quickly and conveniently handled by winches and furling gears instead of by tackles, purchases and muscle.

If winning the occasional race, or getting from one place to another with the least effort in the shortest possible time are the criteria for a cruising yacht, nobody can seriously question the modern design, although it is sometimes said by owners of long-keel, heavy-displacement yachts that the new breed is less safe. This may be true so far as construction and materials are concerned, for sometimes scantlings are pared to a dangerous level, workmanship may be indifferent, and some of the gear shoddy, resulting in failure. It is also said that they are hard to steer before a following sea, and tend to broach-to and get knocked down or even capsized. But I doubt if this happens to them more often than it did to the older type of yacht; it may just be that we hear more of it because there are so very many more of the new type than the old, and they attempt to perform feats undreamed of in the past—and usually succeed. If reassurance about the sea-keeping ability of the modern yacht is needed, we cannot do better than consider the single-handed round the world race, and the Whitbread, in which the competitors kept their vessels going at high speed in appalling weather conditions, and then recall how few of them failed to meet the challenge.

However, as I have stressed earlier in this book, some of us have other criteria which we feel are more important than high speed and brilliant performance to windward, such as the ability to heave-to and nurse the crew in heavy weather, ease of motion in a seaway, ability to carry our not inconsiderable loads of belongings without impairing performance or seaworthiness, gracious yet practical accommodation, and what we in our strange, old-fashioned way regard as good looks. I believe our numbers are swelling, notably in the U.S.A. where an increasing array of 'character' yachts is currently appearing, and where there is a reviving interest in that traditional and well-tried boatbuilding material: good timber.

It is said with some truth that the cockpit and navigation space in the modern yacht is not unlike the flight deck of an aeroplane with its banks of dials and digital readouts. If one racing yacht is so provided her competitors are at a disadvantage unless they also have such aids, but I do sometimes wonder if the coastal cruiser or ocean voyager gains much benefit from such an expensive and often temperamental inventory, though if an owner gets his pleasure that way he should not be denied. My thought is that we who go to sea in small ships might do well to rely, as we did in the past, more on our physical senses than on instruments. The great upsurge of board sailing is the best thing to have happened on the water this decade, and the people who practise the art gain tremendous pleasure and satisfaction from using their physical abilities instead of mechanical or electric aids. Nevertheless, certain instruments are of such great value that once we have used them we would be seriously handicapped without them. The compass is of course essential, though no doubt it was regarded once upon a time as a new-fangled gimmick, and some means of measuring distance run—a towing or impeller log—is important, for neither guessing the speed and thence the distance, nor finding it by timing a chip over a measured distance (the Dutchman's log) is very accurate. The instrument need not incorporate a speed meter, entertaining and instructive though that is in showing instantly the effect of trimming sheets or changing headsails. I regard the echo-sounder as a worthwhile navigation aid if it can be relied on in depths exceeding 10 fathoms (the ones I have owned could not be) for it enables one to follow a contour or obtain a fix by comparing a line of soundings with those shown on the chart. A radio direction-finding set can also be of considerable value, particularly in fog, though the errors to which it and/or its operator are prone need consideration. But do we really require to know, for example, the strength and direction of the wind at the masthead and the yacht's angle to it? The brush of the wind on our cheek or on the back of our neck will probably serve just as well. Nor would I go in for a computer to digest the information provided by the various instruments, for any computer is only as good as the information fed into it, and I have yet to hear of an instrument that will tell one the direction and drift of a current, or the amount of leeway made.

There is, however, one instrument that we would like to have, a satnav. Since Susan and I started making ocean voyages about thirty years ago, we have spent too many dark and anxious nights in the vicinity of low islands or reefs, uncertain of our position because conditions had not been suitable for sun or star observations, and wondering what the current–that great and unpredictable wrecker of ships both large and small–was doing with us. With advancing years we feel that a satnav would do much to ease the tension on such occasions, although we tend to regard its use as a form of cheating. However, we have not yet managed to obtain one for there are delivery and other problems. While thinking about it we were concerned that we might have to run our noisy engine for an additional half an hour each day to provide the current the instrument might need if kept switched on all the time and, as it is, the engine has to be run at sea for an hour a day just to feed the masthead tricolour light. Now we feel that we would probably not use the instrument's ability to keep the dead reckoning up to date, for since we would have to provide the information, some of which would be no more than a guess, we might as well continue to do as we always have and keep the DR on the chart or plotting sheet. The satnav would then only have to be switched on and programmed when approaching dangers or making a landfall in the event that conditions prevented traditional methods of navigation.

*   *   *

While it is heartening to see so many people enjoying the pleasures of sailing and maintaining their vessels, I wish there were fewer of the type that regard a yacht purely as a status symbol, a short term investment, or as a toy only to be played with occasionally, for this has resulted in gross overcrowding in very many places. The late Bill Tilman must have had this in mind when in one of his rare letters to me he wrote, 'Now if you want a good anchorage to yourself you must go into high latitudes,' which was probably why he was bound south on his final voyage with the intention of spending his eightieth birthday in South Georgia. In the past when planning a cruise one selected from the charts suitable, well-sheltered anchorages, but if one does that today as likely as not on arrival one will find the chosen spot choked with moorings occupied by local and often sadly neglected yachts.

Of course it is reasonable that every yacht should have a berth in her home port, pile, swinging or marina, but unfortunately many people do not stop at that and lay other moorings in their favourite places and then rarely use them. I remember this happening long ago in the Beaulieu River where people from the Hamble, who liked to spend occasional weekends off Gins Farm, but who did not care for the bother of anchoring or washing off the mud when weighing, had moorings put down. There were not enough of them seriously to obstruct the anchorage, but one mooring begets others and just look at the place now.

Though laying a mooring may not entitle one to a prior right to that particular bit of sea or river bed, it does prevent its use by others, for nobody in his right mind will lie to a mooring the construction and condition of which is unknown, nor will he anchor so close as to risk fouling it. In some of the more popular parts of New Zealand the indiscriminate laying of moorings in well-sheltered coves, on the shores of which owners have built small holiday homes that stand empty for all but two weeks of the year, has forced the visiting yachts to bring up further from the beach in more exposed positions, or has completely excluded them. Not only individuals but harbour boards also are guilty of this selfish practice. One might well think that the more marinas there are the better, in that they will entice some yachts out of good anchorages and put them into a more compact space in some backwater; but yachts proliferate at such an alarming rate that marinas cannot keep pace with the spate. Steve Dickinson, who owns the Vanisle marina in which we wintered while in British Columbia, told us that if he could get permission to double the size of that marina, every berth would be booked before the first pile had been driven, and I well believe him.

The use of marinas has bred a type of person who does not know how to anchor properly, a failing which is not helped by the common practice, already mentioned, of using a light anchor on a rope cable instead of a suitable one on chain, and if by chance a sufficient scope is veered these yachts sheer about, occupying more than their fair share of space and are a nuisance to everyone nearby – this is one of the penalties paid for light displacement.

Perhaps it is the marina-based mistrust of anchoring, as well as the poor type of ground tackle commonly used, that is the reason why open roadsteads, or passage anchorages as they used often to be called, are not much used now.

In the days of sail when a westerly wind held up traffic bound down the English Channel, many vessels would be found at anchor in the Downs, Dungeness East Road, off St Helens, or in Start Bay or Perran Vose Cove. R. T. McMullen in his book *Down Channel* tells how, in 1886, he in his cutter *Orion* shared the anchorage off Mullion Island in Mounts Bay with more than 80 sailing vessels, all waiting for a hard easterly to abate before attempting to round the Lizard east-bound. He noted how they had arranged themselves according to their ability to make an offing if the wind should come onshore. Nearest the land lay his own yacht and some pilot cutters, then came sloops and yawls and a brig-rigged steamship; outside them lay a row of schooners and ketches, then brigs and barques. Those nearest the land lay quietly, the next lot were rolling a bit, the third group were decidedly uneasy and the outermost, having no protection at all from the island, were rolling miserably. It must have been a wonderful sight.

Since those days, of course, many yachts have made use of passage anchorages, either to shelter from bad weather, to give the crew a rest, or wait for a slant or a favourable tide. However, this is rarely done today, probably because of the almost universal installation of powerful engines which can make light of a contrary tide or perhaps even a fresh headwind, or enable the more gregarious easily to enter a nearby port. This is a pity because a spell in an open and possibly remote anchorage may not only save much time when conditions become favourable for getting under way, but can provide a touch of excitement or adventure on an otherwise uneventful cruise.

Having started my cruising life in yachts which had no auxiliary power, and then having graduated to a yacht with a very small and not too reliable engine, I have spent many a night in, for example, Start Bay in preference to working into Dartmouth, which I have nearly always found to be a difficult undertaking. Today, with the gross overcrowding of most south coast ports and the high dues levied, I think I would still prefer Start Bay.

I had always supposed that there was little risk involved

provided I lay to a single anchor in deep water a sufficient distance from the shore and with a good scope of cable. I knew that if, while I slept, the wind should come onshore, the noise and the motion would wake me in plenty of time to weigh and make an offing before the sea became too rough, and on the only occasion when that was not so the fault was mine—I had stayed there too long.

There is, however, a subtle difference between a passage anchorage in home waters with a safe port within easy reach, and an open anchorage off some lonely coast exposed to the full fetch of an ocean. One of the latter kind which we used a good many years ago was Loughros More on the west coast of Ireland. Bound north in our 30-foot sloop we had left Killybegs one lovely June morning with the hope of making an anchorage at Rutland Harbour among the Rosses, a distance of about 40 miles. The wind was light from the east as we made our way along that splendid cliffy coast and we ate our lunch as we passed inside Rathlin O'Birne. But progress grew slower and slower as the wind fell lighter and drew ahead. By evening the wind had fallen right away and Susan suggested that we motor to near-by Loughros More Bay and spend the night there. This we did over the shining sea which had not a ripple on it. Just as the distorted orb of the sun fell into the sea, so we let the anchor go in five fathoms, and when the purr of the engine died away there was no sound but the sad, slow sigh of the swell breaking on the distant beach, a beach which at one end gives way to an estuary of which the *Pilot* says: 'The swell is generally so heavy that in summer a boat might not be able to cross the bar for several weeks, and in winter seldom.' The glass was high and steady, and the night we spent at anchor in that bay was peaceful. But some fishermen we met later were shocked when they heard we had been there, for it has a bad reputation and apparently a heavy swell can rise suddenly and without warning.

In some respect Loughros More is similar to a bay in New Zealand called Little Omaha which we recently used, but whereas Loughros faces west to the North Atlantic, Omaha faces east to the South Pacific. All day while coming 50 miles south along the coast we had been closehauled in a wind of 30 knots with stronger gusts, which had forced us further offshore than we had intended. It was getting rough out there, we were salt-caked and weary and clearly were not going to reach Kawau Island, our intended destination, before dark. The channel we would have to take to get there is not easy by night, and since we knew that not long ago vandals had twisted the light on its pillar so that the narrow white sector shone over rocks instead of through the passage, and might have done so again, we tacked and stood in towards Omaha. As we closed the land and came within the bay's embrace, the shouting wind moderated, and by the time we let the anchor go two miles inside the headlands it had dropped to a light, offshore breeze.

Because of the low sun and the glare off the water in our eyes we could not distinguish features of the shore very well, but could see that the beach was of sand and was backed by low sandhills. On the starboard bow the chart showed an estuary, just as at Loughros, but this we could not make out, though after dark some lights appeared in that direction. After a peaceful night in the bay, which we had thought to be a wild and lonely place, it was something of a disappointment when the early morning sun, clearly illuminating the land, showed that the shores of the estuary were lined with a jostle of little, low houses, holiday 'baches' in which New Zealanders delight. From where we lay the place looked not unlike the Arab fishing village of Faqum, Gulf of Aden, off which we had once lain, another open anchorage. The keen sense of remoteness which we had savoured on arrival had vanished with daylight, so we got our hook and moved on to Kawau.

In the trade wind areas of the world open anchorages are common. At St Helena and Ascension in the South Atlantic, for example, the only anchorages are open and of course in the lee of those islands and since the wind there is constantly from the east or south-east they are safe throughout the year. But because of the swell that rolls in they are far from comfortable, and landing at the flights of steps provided for the purpose can be a wet and hilarious undertaking. On our first visit to Ascension some twenty years ago the manager of the cable station insisted that we move ashore and live in his big, cool house for the three days of our stay because our little vessel was rolling so violently.

Sometimes, however, the anchorage in the lee of a trade wind island can be quite comfortable. I recall lying in a bay on the west (lee) side of Tahuata, one of the Marquesas, and at that time there were 14 overseas yachts there, most of them under different flags—it was like a cosmopolitan floating village. For us one of the great pleasures and interests has been meeting the other voyagers when in port, and we used to make a point of calling on everyone with whom we were sharing an anchorage. But today there are so many—about 150 overseas yachts put in at our home port each year before the South Pacific hurricane season starts—that we can no longer do so. However, at Tahuata most of us called on one another by dinghy and landed on the beach without difficulty to pick fruit. Meanwhile the eastern port of entry for the group, only 10 miles away in Hiva Oa, was reported to be experiencing such a heavy swell that several dinghies were capsized while attempting to effect a landing, and others were swept away.

However, one cannot rely everywhere on the trade wind blowing from the right direction all the time. While cruising for some weeks among the many islands of Vanuatu, again and again we had to leave open, recommended anchorages because the trade died away and was replaced by an onshore wind. Apparently this was an unusual happening, and was probably due to a huge band of thunderstorms which at the time extended in a north and south direction for more than a thousand miles.

Looking back over the years I realise that the majority of occasions on which Susan and I have made use of open anchorages were pleasant enough. In spite of the wide open horizon of some ocean, and though perhaps with a little swell, we rested in them and for the most part enjoyed the feeling of isolation, perhaps even of vulnerability. But there were two occasions when conditions were abominable.

During one of our voyages from England to the South Pacific we had, on leaving Panama, made our way up the west coast of Central America bound towards San Diego in California. Although the coastwise trip was an interesting experience, for we called at many places, we would have done much better from a sailing point of view to have gone first to the westward to connect with the route from the Horn. Inshore the prevailing wind is north or north-west, a headwind, and the current flows south-east against one. However, thanks largely to a reliable engine of sufficient power, we managed to creep north (the 3,025 miles took 72 days including stopovers) and by late April were on the final stage with San Diego only a few days away. Coming along that coast we always tried to make our northing in the forenoons, for the afternoon wind usually freshened to such a degree that we could make little progress against it. It was on one such boisterous afternoon that, unable to proceed further, we anchored in desolate Colnett Bay on the Mexican coast. Neither on the chart nor in fact did this look much of an anchorage, but it was the only one we could make. Punta Colnett, a strange, flat-topped, vertical-sided, semi-circular headland, did just protect us from the rough and crested sea, but it did nothing to guard us from the ocean swell which rolled unhindered into the bay and, measured by echo-sounder after we had anchored, had a height of six to seven feet. Each swell, having lifted and dropped us, exploded with an awful roar on the beach which, due to the curve of the bay and the direction of the wind, then lay close astern.

Instead of the wind easing in the night, as it usually did, it freshened more, and the gusts which came swooping down from that remarkable headland exceeded 40 knots. You may well wonder why we endured such a situation when the whole Pacific with its deep, safe water lay beside us. The reason was that some days before I had smashed my thumb rather badly and was still feeling ill and unfit to continue for long at sea. Fearful that the cable might catch short on a rock, snub and part, Susan kept an anxious watch through the night while I cowered in my bunk.

In the morning we got away and tried to round the headland, which seemed to go on and on interminably, but wind and sea were too much for us. Of course we ought to have stood out to sea, but instead we foolishly returned to spend a further 24 hours in the bay, where our feeling of apprehension was heightened by the presence of a grey whale which swam close round us for a long time.

The other open anchorage which neither of us will ever forget was in South Africa near Cape St Francis. For several weeks we had been imprisoned in a river which we ought never to have entered, for its bar had insufficient water for us even at high tide. However, at last we had managed to escape. The large bay into which the river flows is entirely open between north-east and south-east, i.e. to the Indian Ocean, but provides excellent shelter from the west and south. The wind was west, and as we were bound in that direction we anchored for the night and to await a fair wind.

During the night the swell built up to set us rolling, and at dawn, with rain, the wind shifted to the south. As the forecast was for freshening westerlies, I assumed that the wind shift was a temporary one (though I should have been warned by the swell) and decided to hang on. But instead of going back to the west, as predicted, the wind shifted the other way, to the south-east, and by mid-morning we no longer had any shelter. Of course we had to get out, but that took longer than it should have done for our anchor was foul of some obstruction, possibly a rock, and we had great difficulty recovering it. Meanwhile the swell had built with astonishing speed into quite a heavy sea, and as we motor-sailed out of the bay one particularly steep roller swept us from stem to stern carrying away some loose gear and distorting the supports of the cockpit hood. That night, as we ran before a sustained gale of 65 knots under bare poles, we felt almost light-hearted, not only at having escaped from the river but from near disaster in Cape St Francis Bay.

The contrasts of cruising are memorable and one of its greater attractions. Recently we spent a night in a lovely little cove set among softly rounded green hills on the East coast of New Zealand's North Island. The entrance is open to the east-nor'east, and from the anchorage one can look out towards Panama, which is more than 6,000 miles distant. The wind did not come from that direction, however, indeed there was no wind under the overcast sky, nor was there any glimmer of light from the shore which is uninhabited. The only sounds were the whisper of a slight surge among the rocks, the soft 'plop' of a fish breaking surface and the call of a distant more port owl.

*   *   *

I have been reading in an American magazine a story by a man who claims he enjoys calms. This astonished me, yet he must have known what he was writing about as he had sailed for some years and had at least one Atlantic crossing to his credit. A calm on a summer's evening in some river or absolutely smooth body of water, when one can listen to the voices of the birds and watch the sunset colours flush then fade, can be delightful for a short time, but for me a calm at sea is an abomination hard to endure, though not because of the lack of progress.

On our various voyages Susan and I have experienced many calms, some of them lasting for several days; but no matter how long they did last there was always some left-over sea running, or a swell perhaps from a disturbance many hundreds of miles away, and the resulting motion was enough to slam the sails unmercifully from side to side no matter how light they were or how hard-sheeted. The noise we have come to dread more than any other is the sudden shuddering crash and the harsh machine gun rattle of slides on mast and boom as the belly of the mainsail slams to and fro with explosive force, subjecting itself to more strain and general wear than any gale could cause. Mast, rigging, and sometimes the whole ship vibrate as the drunken masthead sock swings wildly round and round its stick; we cannot endure it for more than a few minutes, so the sail has to be taken in. That is a job we detest and sometimes fear, as the slamming Terylene tries to snatch the gaskets from our hands and slaps our faces as we position them and until it can be tamed, the halyard beats savagely against the resounding mast. At least the stout boom gallows, which we have had in all our yachts, is a considerable help on such occasions. On some passages south of the trade wind belt and before the westerlies are met with, where the wind seems to be more fluky than it is in other parts of the open oceans, often blowing at Force 5 or 6 for a short time, then dying right away only to return soon after, we have taken the mainsail in and reset it as many as a dozen times in a single day—a frustrating and wearisome business. With no sail to help steady her, the ship's motion becomes even more violent and jerky; everything that can move moves, including fuel and water which rush noisily from side to side in their tanks. I believe the multi-hull is less violent in her antics in such conditions, and possibly some light-displacement, fin-keel yachts are too. I have no proof of this, but I notice that the crews of such yachts do not complain about calms so bitterly as I do.

Sometimes our impatient and almost instant handing of the mainsail has turned out to be a bad move. A few days ago we were running for Cuvier Island before a strong wind and rough sea under the deeply-reefed mainsail. In the evening the wind came more abeam and moderated, so we set the staysail and unrolled the reefs, but only to be left becalmed and slamming horribly soon after. As usual we took the mainsail in, but an hour later the wind was back once more, and immediately blew so hard that we did not believe we would be able to set the sail and then reef it without either damaging it or ourselves, and of course we could not reef the sail down to a manageable size before setting it—that was the only occasion when the pendant and point reefing, which we had abandoned in Australia in favour of roller gear, might have served us well. So all through that dark and windy night the only sail we had set was the little staysail, though we were able to use part of the jib later, and did not get the main up until Cuvier Island drew near at dawn. Perhaps we should have reefed the slamming sail before we took it down, but how could we have known? And there are limits to the amount of sail handling we can undertake.

The modern marine diesel engine, if it is provided with its simple basic diet of air, cooling water, and clean fuel and oil, is a remarkably willing and long-lasting friend, so today, when a yacht is becalmed at sea, the tendency is to hand all sail and motor on. This is another of the changes in outlook that have taken place in recent years, and no doubt the headway made through the water has a partial steadying effect. In *Wanderer IV*, with her sturdy Ford in its sound-proofed engine-room and a bountiful supply of fuel, we took to using the engine when becalmed more and more as we grew older, and at times motored on relentlessly. But in *V*, with her smaller amd much more noisy engine, I feel a certain reluctance to let the little diesel grind away hour after hour when out of sight of land, preferring to husband it for more important occasions. Nevertheless, we usually come to running it in the end and pray, meanwhile, that the wind will soon return while we keep our weather eyes lifting for the first catspaw to darken the pale and shiny surface of the sea. And what a relief and delight it is when at last a worthwhile breeze fills in, the sails are up and pulling silently, and a musical chuckle comes from the forefoot. But just fancy anybody claiming to *enjoy* a calm!

Since the trend among voyaging yachts today is to make considerable use of the engine when on passage, not only in calms but sometimes to make progress against headwinds, the traditional question asked by those in a dinghy from a nearby yacht which has recently made the same passage, as they come alongside with a gift of fruit or cold beer, 'How many days?' is now almost a thing of the past, for passage times can no longer be compared unless the number of engine hours and the horsepower are known.

*   *   *

I once met a man who told me that he always planned his passages so as to have the benefit of the moon at any difficult point and when making a landfall. I don't know how he managed this unless he used his engine a great deal or spent a lot of time hove-to waiting, for although most of us in heavily-laden non-racing types of voyaging yachts reckon on averaging something a little more than 100 miles a day on an ocean crossing, we cannot bank on it. For instance, the fifth time Susan and I crossed the North Atlantic from east to west we took 36 days instead of the 25 or so of earlier trips, and a recent 1,000-mile passage from Suva to North Cape, which we had on another occasion, but at the same time of year, done in less than 8 days, this time took us 19.

Nevertheless the moon-man's idea stood him in good stead on at least one occasion. At the end of his first Atlantic crossing he made a landfall on Barbados, but apparently there had been some confusion over the lights of that island, which he was planning to round on its northern side. He was under power at the time and fortunately had organised the moon properly, for it was by the light of the moon that he sighted breakers ahead and saved his ship by promptly going astern.

As we lie in a well-sheltered river inhabited by terns, cormorants, gulls and kingfishers, I sometimes think of the fleets of ocean voyagers gathering at certain staging points along their chosen routes waiting for the moon, and particularly just now for the moon is waxing. We recently had a letter from American friends, written at Port Moresby, telling us that, with two other yachts, they were waiting for the moon before setting out to thread their way among the reefs and islets of the Great Northeast Channel en route for Torres Strait and the Indian Ocean. It was not so many weeks ago that they were anchored close to us just prior to their departure from New Zealand, and efficient and competent navigators though they are they were clearly a little apprehensive about the approaches to Torres Strait; that was as it should be, for it is usually those who take such awkward stretches casually and without proper thought or plan who find themselves in difficulties.

They told us that the local tug skipper, an Australian, was going to hold a seminar for the crews of the yachts before they left; that was a kindly thought, but I wonder if it can be of much help, for their major problem will be to find the low speck of land called Bramble Cay, which marks the entry to the Northeast Channel when one is approaching from the east. I doubt if local knowledge can be of much assistance there, but only accurate navigation. Even then, as many a navigator has discovered, the strong and variable currents in the neighbourhood of the cay can be defeating. An 11-mile light stands on the cay, but I think it must be of very low power, for on three occasions we have been quite close to it in the dark without sighting it, though once we saw its latticework structure shortly after dawn. With this in mind I begin to wonder if they were wise to wait for full moon, as a low-power light is more readily seen on a dark night. However, at least one thing should make their trip towards Bramble Cay a little less anxious than ours had been: the vigia known to generations of seamen as Goldie Reef, said to be awash at low water and lying on the direct route from Port Moresby to Bramble Cay, has—so we learnt from the skipper of the lighthouse tender at Thursday Island the last time we passed through—been disproved and deleted from the chart.

Over many years laborious searches have failed to find many of the reported dangers shown on the Pacific charts, and presumably every now and then survey or other vessels feel sufficiently confident of their investigations which disprove the existence of one for it to be deleted subsequently from the chart, as with Goldie Reef, for example. Another, which in the past caused us some concern, but which has also now vanished from the up-to-date chart, used to be marked about 100 miles west of the northern end of Tonga. It was reported more recently than most, in 1944, when its western end was said to be five feet high and its eastern end submerged but marked by breakers. In the ordinary way one should have no reason for going near it, but we had been blown away from Vava'u by a long-lasting gale of considerable violence, and to avoid being driven upon the active volcano of Fanua Lai, which lay under our lee, we streamed a sea-anchor over the stern to reduce the yacht's speed and enable her to steer herself with wind and sea on the quarter, and so go clear. After spending four days like that we were not at all sure of the dead reckoning, for continuous overcast and rain had prevented the taking of sights (you see why we are thinking of getting a satnav) but we believed we were getting somewhere near the danger. Then, fortunately for us, the gale blew itself out and we were able to make sail and steer what we hoped was a safe course. Now it seems that danger was only a myth, perhaps reported by some vessel who was not where she thought she was, or had sighted jumping fish or cetacians, a patch of pumice, a mass of plankton, or possibly just the shadow of a cloud. However none of these, which again and again have been the cause of suspected dangers being reported and marked on the chart, could account for the 'five foot high' description.

In only one respect are vigias to be commended. In these days when, for many people with the necessary equipment, navigation has been made so simple and accurate and when so many voyaging yachts have adequate power and fuel, perhaps it is no bad thing now and then for a skipper to be anxious about a vigia, possibly terrified of it, even though he may have taken the doubtful precaution of heaving-to during the hours of darkness. He will then experience for a little while some of the anxieties and problems with which his forefathers were so often confronted while exploring those waters in unhandy square-riggers.

As the moon waxes our thoughts turn also to the Marquesas where another, but larger, bunch of voyagers no doubt has gathered, nearly all of them bound for Tahiti by way of the Tuamotu, that vast maze of reefs and atolls which is sometimes known as the 'Dangerous Archipelago'. They, too, will be waiting for the voyagers' moon. I believe this is wise, for there are virtually no lights to look for in the Tuamotu, and it might so happen that if the moon were in the right place at the right time her light could show a danger early enough for avoiding action to be taken. Also, by illuminating the horizon, the moon may on occasions permit star observations to be taken at times other than twilight, and she herself might be the means of providing a valuable position line.

Hundreds of small sailing vessels scattered over the waters within the tropics will at this time be waiting for the full moon to shed her maximum light throughout the 12-hour night to help them navigate difficult waters; even for those who may have no immediate navigational problems, the silver light from the moon with the big, smiling face will be a comfort and a delight for many a night watchkeeper. As Ann Pye put it:

> 'There's magic in the moonlight,
> Adventures in our lee . . .'

Although all yacht navigators make use of the sun, and most of them use the stars as well, there seems to be a certain reluctance to use the moon, yet she can be of great help, particularly in daylight, when a position line obtained from her can be crossed straightaway with a position line obtained from the sun so as to give a fix.

Since a moon observation is worked in the same manner as is a sun or planet observation, I suggest that the general reluctance may be due indirectly to the thought of what Lecky refers to as 'so many petty and vexatious corrections which spin the calculations out to a weary length'. But since he wrote his classic *Wrinkles in Practical Navigation* the matter has been much simplified, so that to obtain the true altitude from the sextant reading calls for little more correction than is needed with any other body, and the more often we do it the quicker we become.

The moon is growing fat and round now and when, last night, I watched her sailing over the scrub-covered hills which enclose our present snug retreat, I thought of our friends on their way to Bramble Cay, of others among the Tuamotu, and of the countless little ships all over the globe seeking their landfalls and looking, perhaps a little anxiously, for moonlit dangers—and I wished them cloudless skies.

*   *   *

Moorea in French Polynesia is not only the most spectacular small island that Susan and I know, but it offers excellent anchorages in both of the fiordlike inlets that thrust into its northern coast; good water can be had there, most simple provisions including wine and French bread are available at the Chinese stores, and after one has got off the busy perimeter road there are delightful walks to be had inland through the valleys, where the red/brown winding road contrasts pleasantly with the lush, green vegetation, and on all sides jaunty mountain peaks, some between 3,000 and 4,000 feet in height, stand stark against the blue sky or appear mysteriously through swirling clouds. We decided that Moorea would make an excellent objective for our 1984 cruise in the South Pacific, and an added incentive was that one of our friends from Canada, Steve Dickinson, had planned to sail there in his handsome Garden-designed ketch *Kapduva*, and was going to leave San Diego in California at about the same time as we would be leaving New Zealand. What fun it would be if we suddenly turned up at Moorea to surprise him and renew our friendship!

We wished to make the voyage to Polynesia direct. It may be recalled that we had attempted this as *Wanderer V*'s maiden voyage, and that because of bad weather and a number of defects that showed up in our new ship, we aborted the trip and went instead to much nearer and easier Fiji. This rankled, for it was the first time we had abandoned a major sailing project; so for our satisfaction and self-respect we must try again, and this time succeed. Of course the passage would be a repetition of the one we had made in *Wanderer IV* when on our way to the west coast of Canada, in that we would keep to much the same track and make our easting in the variables which lie between the south-east trade wind and the boisterous westerlies that predominate south of 40°S. However, no two voyages along the same track are ever quite alike as Kipling knew so well when he wrote:

> But we're back once more on the old trail, our own trail, the out trail,
> We're down, hull down, on the Long Trail–the trail that is always new!

On this trip we thought it would be interesting to try out one of the modern satellite navigation systems to which I referred earlier. We would then be keeping up with the Joneses as well as improving our education, and on the return trip by way of island groups we hoped it might be of real assistance on occasions when fixes by observations of sun, moon or stars were impossible.

The only satnavs readily available in New Zealand were Japanese-made; they were reported on favourably, but the owner of one told us that the instructions were not written in the kind of English that English-speaking people understand. I knew exactly what he meant, for we had owned two Japanese engines and the instructions that came with them were poor, did not use current engineering terms, and were illustrated with childish drawings showing little men presumably doing all the right things.

We tried for a Walker, but it never came, and at the eleventh hour, as it were, we ordered a Magnavox direct from the U.S.A. As we were due to sail on 1 April we said it must be on a plane by 15 March–and it was. Customs had advised us that we might have it free of duty provided that on our cruise we were out of the country for six months, so it came as a considerable shock to be told by a more senior official when we went to get the instrument from the bond store, that unless we stayed away for twenty-one months we would be charged 98% duty (roughly $NZ 3000) on our return.

It did not take long to install the instrument, for we had done in advance the preliminary work of erecting a post to hold the antenna in the stern, and running a gantline through the deck and bulkheads and along a stringer to the place where the console was to be, so that the coaxial cable could be pulled through at once. American friends who had a similar instrument, and indeed had been largely responsible for us getting ours, kindly came aboard to give us a few hints and do two small soldering jobs.

I found the instruction manual, a book of some 90 large pages, difficult to understand, for it appeared to have been written not for beginners like me but for those who already had some understanding of computers and the terms used with them. No doubt any modern boy or girl would have mastered it within an hour or two, but I knew that I could never do so in the few days remaining, so I did not even try, claiming that I had too many other things to attend to. However, Susan persevered to the extent that by the time we sailed she could get the instrument to provide a fix, which of course was what we had bought it for, but she never got round to persuading it to do its other tricks, such as giving the course and distance between two points, ETA, etc. I promised myself that during the forthcoming voyage I would learn how to operate the Magnavox even though it might be more complicated than some, having 36 keys instead of the 26 of most other makes. Incidentally, I wondered, and still do, what the significance (if any) is of the figures 4 and 2. Walkers called their first model the 402 and their second the 412; Magnavox call theirs 4102.

There were lots of calms and light headwinds during the first week of the voyage, and on thirteen occasions we took in the sails because we could not put up with their dreadful slamming as we rolled in the swell. I do not know if our present vessel's motion is worse than that of her predecessors about which I often complained, but she certainly flings herself about, and after a 2-second roll recovers with a jerk which is hard on her gear and her crew. There were some days when we made no easting at all. Then, heralded by sinister displays of cirrus and solar haloes, two deep depressions which were travelling much farther north than they usually do unless of tropical origin, overtook us with winds in excess of 50 knots. When those winds were fair we made some worthwhile progress, but when they blew from ahead we did not, and on one occasion we remained hove-to for forty-eight despondent hours. As a result of these backs our runs for the first three weeks were only 449, 537 607 miles.

For much of the time there was low, damp cloud and often intermittent rain, so I got few opportunities for checking that the satnav, of which I then had some mistrust, was doing its job properly; but when I was able to practise the old art with sextant and tables it was reassuring to find that the satnav and I agreed we were in the same part of the ocean, so confidence in the new acquisition increased. Because the wind was so variable in strength and direction it was not possible to feed the instrument with the accurate course and speed it required. Had we stood proper deck watches and steered by hand instead of leaving that entirely to the vane gear, this information could have been more precise, though it would have called for frequent changes to be entered, and we began to understand the advantages of having a speedometer and compass interfaced with the Magnavox. We had not invested in those extras because of the added cost and complication and the need for an additional skin fitting; nor had I thought them important at the time of ordering, being of the opinion then that all we required from the satnav was a fix once a day or more often when near dangers, and had not understood that in the event of the dead reckoning (DR) position being more than 20 miles in error (though this is not common it can happen, particularly during long periods of calm) the next fix by satellite will be inaccurate, and subsequent fixes even more so, unless one 'forces an update', but we could not understand from the manual how to do that.

On our 12-volt supply the Magnavox consumes one amp, and if kept switched on continually would call for one hour's charging of the ship's batteries each day; so except when about to make a landfall we kept it running only for a few hours each day just to get familiar with its operation. Also, with the conservation of electricity in mind, we did not use the masthead tricolour light, which would have called for another hour a day of charging, but hung our big paraffin-burning, dioptric-lens riding light between the backstay legs on a bar I had fitted there for the purpose; from that position its powerful beam shone unobstructed all round, passing over the cockpit hood and beneath the boom.

It is sometimes thought that satnav will provide a fix at any moment one wants it to, but this is not so. It will keep the DR going so long as it is provided with the course and speed, and it will update the DR each time it obtains a fix from a satellite. But there are at times quite long intervals between satellite passes, depending in part on where the ship is. In about 30°S, 160°W, for example, we could get no fix between midnight and 0500. There is also the possibility that when the instrument does acquire a satellite it may reject it for one or more of nine reasons, and by means of a code it tells one the reason for rejection. Indeed, it tells one all sorts of things such as GMT and LMT to the second, and the supercilious manner in which it displays ? ? ? ? ? when one has made some silly mistake is almost human.

Beyond the fact that we wished to find some warmer and drier place in which to winter among the islands, we had not told anyone of our intentions, and the knowledge that in the event we were never seen or heard of again not a soul would know what we were attempting and nobody could possibly initiate an air/sea search, gave us a pleasurable feeling of independence, which perhaps was heightened a little by the emptiness of the ocean across which we forged our lonely track. Except on the final night when we were approaching land we saw no other vessel throughout the 31 days the 2,634-mile passage took, but at times we could listen in to U.K. and N.Z. radio stations on short wave and get the news, but often this pleasure was denied us because of the atmospherics caused on many days by thunder.

We saw very little wildlife, but we did have a touching visit by some swallows when we were only a few days out and south of the Kermadecs. Possibly their navigation systems had broken down or they were running low on stores, for three of those courageous long-distance voyagers came aboard. One of them perched on one of the vane gear's steering lines dangerously close to the block through which it was working, and had to be removed before its toes got trapped. Another, while in the cabin, perched on the book Susan was reading. They showed no fear or distrust of us. Usually visits by land birds are sad affairs, and particularly so with swallows, for one cannot feed them with the insects that form their diet, nor can one persuade them to drink anything. So the longer they remain the more exhausted do they become, and in the morning there is probably a small dead body to be disposed of. At least Susan was able to make the final few hours for one of the birds more comfortable than they might otherwise have been, for she bedded it down on a soft duster in a corner of the chart-table.

We had learnt that Bora Bora, one of the Society Islands lying about 150 miles west-nor'west of Tahiti, was now a port of entry, so we chose to go there instead of to dirty, noisy, discourteous Papeete, the capital of French Polynesia for which we have little affection; as soon as we deemed it prudent to do so (in about 158°W) we began to slant nor'nor'east towards that island, and a few evenings later the Plough was visible upside down in the northern sky. In the forenoon of our 28th day at sea we sailed close past Rimatara, one of the Austral Group; but as that island has no harbour, lagoon or reasonable anchorage we did not stop, and Susan celebrated the occasion by baking bread, which we ate hot for lunch. Only then did we come into better and more settled weather with a healthy-looking sky and a steady wind which gave us the best day's run of the passage— 146 miles.

Confidence in the Magnavox had now increased to the point that we had no hesitation in approaching Bora Bora by night, something we would scarcely have done on the strength of a pair of indifferent sun sights taken the previous day, and in the first faint light of dawn three days after passing Rimatara, there ahead stood the well-remembered twin peaks dominating the motu-circled lagoon in which the island stands, and farther off to starboard lay the mountains of Raiatea. The swell was thundering on the reef as we sailed to the wide and easy pass, and by breakfast time we lay at anchor near a gathering of other yachts off the Oa Oa hotel, and were still.

The owner/manager of the hotel has a liking for voyaging people, and at his excellent dinghy landing has erected a notice welcoming them. Water and showers are available, and these like the moorings, of which he has laid several, are free. No doubt this is why most visiting yachts choose to lie there, though the anchorage is deep (14–16 fathoms) and is a little uneasy when the trade wind is fresh.

For most of our stay we lay, as we had in the past, in the lee of uninhabited Toopua Island where the water is smooth and only 5 fathoms deep, and one can look out across a mile of vivid thinly covered reef to the breakers at its seaward edge and watch the sun set behind them. Shortly before leaving New Zealand the American makers of our defective echo-sounder had kindly sent us an improved model, which we installed, but we had not changed the transducer because we did not want a gush of water in the dry bilge where many things were stowed. We now took the opportunity while lying in smooth, warm water to do this without making a mess. Susan dived down, and having found the transducer placed her hand over it and signalled with a tap on the hull; I at once unscrewed the collar and pulled out the old transducer (not a drop of water came in) but before inserting the new one I poked my finger in the hole to make sure it was clean, and there encountered something soft and wrinkled. For a moment I thought a jellyfish had taken up residence, but of course it was only the palm of Susan's hand. Quickly I popped in the new transducer and tapped on the hull to let Susan know I had done, and she surfaced with very little breath left. After that the sounder worked much better, but it failed to register above 22 fathoms although it is supposed to go up to 60.

While we lay by Toopua Island there was another incident, and a rather alarming one. The trade had died and for several days there had been puffs of wind from all directions driving us over and round our anchor again and again. With the thought that the chain might have fouled it, we decided to sight the 60-lb CQR. We were lying to 30 fathoms of cable and had got in about half of that when the anchor came to the surface with the remaining 15 fathoms of chain hanging in a bight from it. With slip-ropes and some cunning we sorted out the mess and re-anchored. An hour later the wind came fresh onshore, and with torrential rain blotting out everything more than a ship's length away, rose to 35 knots. Thankful that we had cleared the anchor before this happened, we were standing drenched in the cockpit when we saw milky water very close astern. This must be the island's fringing reef and the anchor is dragging, were our immediate thoughts. At once we started the engine, weighed the anchor, which in fact had a very good hold, and motored to windward. But the 'reef' astern was just as close as before, and then with great relief we realised that the dis-coloured water was no reef, but was the run-off from the island caused by the tremendous downpour of rain.

The passage to Moorea was a 130-mile beat into the trade wind and a short, steep, confused and most uncomfortable sea. At dawn of the second day the island lay close ahead, and quite becalmed we motored into Papetoai, the nearest of the two inlets on the north coast, and anchored near its head on the eastern side which was still in the morning shadow of the mountains; the scent of freshly-cut grass drifted out from the homestead where Mr Kellum (probably the oldest and longest-established settler on the island) was mowing his lawns. There were only two other yachts in sight, and they like ourselves were wearing plain red ensigns—surely a rare happening today in those largely American-dominated waters.

We remained for two nights, then went round to the next inlet where we found *Kapduva* with Steve Dickinson aboard. She had sailed the 3,740 miles from San Diego in 36 days, and had only just arrived in Moorea. Clearly Steve was surprised to see us, but I believe he got as much pleasure as we did from this meeting of the two ships from such widely-separated ports, a meeting that had only been hinted at in letters written months before.

Index